PARIS
CONFIDENTIAL
2000-2001

Assouline Publishing
601 West 26th Street, New York, NY 10001
Tel: 212-989-6810   Fax: 212-647-0005
www.assouline.com

First published in French by Éditions Assouline
Paris confidentiel 2000-2001 © 2000 Éditions Assouline
English translation by Christina Henry de Tessan
© 2000 Éditions Assouline
Copy editing: Leigh Anna Mendenhall

Distributed to the US trade by St. Martin's Press
and in Canada by McClelland & Stewart

ISBN: 2 84323 189 2

Printed in Italy

Anne-Cécile Sanchez & Cédric Reversade

PARIS
CONFIDENTIAL
2000-2001

ASSOULINE

PARIS
CHAOS
CONFIDENTIAL
2000-2001

Paris Confidential describes an unexpected and contemporary Paris not featured in traditional tourist guides. Stylish, funny, and glamorous, it reveals a Paris of both known quantities and new trends.

Because you don't merely want the facts (eating, drinking, and sleeping), but also the mood and character of the places you visit, we describe the light, the atmosphere, the people. And we offer a range—from indispensable, well-known addresses to our latest finds.

Paris, the capital of *la gastronomie?* Yes, a thousand times, yes! But we also describe Paris and its cafés, Paris and its artists and designers, the Paris of night owls, Paris in action....

Give free reign to your desires. Here are the little known museums, leading galleries, trendy record stores, florists, hairdressers, markets, clothing boutiques, dance classes, swimming pools, turkish baths, gardens, old movie theaters, clubs—and much, much more.

There are so many ways to make the most of your time here and experience the charms of this clandestine Paris. *Bon voyage!!*

Anne-Cécile Sanchez and Cédric Reversade

Table of Contents

ROOMS

Rooms]

Because luxury is not only determined by the thickness of carpets and double curtains, but also by the size of the rooms, the crunch of the gravel in the interior courtyard, the discreet elegance of the furniture or the guests, the establishments that we have selected—priced between 300 and 3000 francs (46–457 €)—all appealed to us for their charm. And if it's a modest hotel? We chose it for its cheerful setting, perfect location, or efficient and friendly staff. Even if we haven't exactly "discovered" the four-star hotels, we have selected the most sumptuous and extraordinary among them. Finally, if you've decided to set your bags down in a family-style boarding house, we invite you to take advantage of the luxury palaces for tea or a cocktail.

1st arrondissement

HÔTEL COSTES / *Chic and luxurious*
239, rue Saint-Honoré, 1st arr., M° Concorde
Tel. : 01.42.44.50.00 – fax : 01.42.44.50.01
www.hotelcostes.com

Even if the palace of Versailles is still where it's always been, the royalty now gathers at the Hôtel Costes; since its opening, number 239 of the rue Saint-Honoré has been the address of choice for the press, film industry, and fashion world. With its vast patio decorated with an antique portico, red and bronze velour-lined sitting rooms, and soft lighting, it's *the* meeting place for beautiful people and one of the wildest spots in the capital. This small gem decorated by Jacques Garcia links the opulence and precociousness of imperial style with a modern, affluent level of comfort. The overall effect is a bit rococo—lots of fringes and pompons—and a bit frenetic at peak times, but extremely refined overall. For tea, choose the sitting room with the fireplace, and, if you are reserving a room, be sure to ask for one with a mini-terrace—a divine treat on summer mornings. From 1750 francs (266,80 €).

HÔTEL HENRI IV / *Minimalist*
25, place Dauphine, 1st arr., M° Pont-Neuf, Cité, Saint-Michel
Tel. : 01.43.54.44.53

Where can you find a room in the heart of Paris for under 300 francs (46 €)? Mission impossible is the answer you'll get from most. However, the impossible does exist, tucked away in the place Dauphine. American professors in Paris for conferences at the Sorbonne stay here regularly, spartan though it may be—the notion of comfort here being limited to the bare minimum. But what a luxury to stay a few steps from Saint-Germain-des-Prés and the Île de la Cité in a bright room with a shower and windows that open onto one of the loveliest and most serene squares in the city! Remember, however, to reserve at least four weeks ahead.

HÔTEL MANSART / *Overlooking the place Vendôme*
5, rue des Capucines, 1st arr., M° Opéra
Tel. : 01.42.61.50.28 – fax : 01.49.27.97.44
hotel.mansart@wanadoo.fr

Despite a somewhat dissuasive entry hall, two major assets caused us to list this hotel generally mobbed during business conferences: the astonishing size of two of its comfortable and classic high-ceiling rooms and its breathtaking view overlooking the place Vendôme. Two steps from the Ritz, the

Mansart obviously doesn't belong in the same category, but for under 1000 francs (152,45 €), you'll enjoy the pleasant feeling of having a vast *pied-à-terre* in a large bourgeois home. From 750 francs (114,34 €).

HÔTEL MEURICE / *Sumptuous Renaissance*
228, rue de Rivoli, 1st arr., M° Tuileries
Tel.: 01.44.58.10.10 – fax: 01.44.58.10.19
www.meuricehotel.com

After several months of ambitious renovation, the Meurice—one of the bastions of fine Parisian hotellery—will re-open its doors this year. Even if we can't say anything definitive for the moment, we're awaiting the restoration of the palace's belle époque glasswork as a major event. To have tea here under its natural light is going to be a must for sun-filled spring and summer afternoons. From 2950 francs (449,72 €).

5th arrondissement

ESMERALDA / *A bit shabby...but what a view!*
4, rue Saint-Julien-le-Pauvre, 5th arr., M° Saint-Michel
Tel.: 01.43.54.19.20 – fax: 01.40.51.00.68

Facing Notre-Dame, the Esmerelda is almost as well-known as the gothic cathedral itself, and a godsend that the natives will surely tell you about even if few have actually stayed there. In this seventeenth-century building, the view and winding staircase are well-preserved and the prices are fixed (twenty rooms with baths at under 500 francs or 76 €). You'll also have to accept the rickety furniture, aged bedding, and the persistent sound of traffic on the river bank below...but the charm of old Paris is certainly to be found!

HÔTEL DES GRANDES ÉCOLES / *Floral provincial*
75, rue du Cardinal-Lemoine, 5th arr., M° Cardinal-Lemoine
Tel.: 01.43.26.79.23 – fax: 01.43.26.67.32
www.hotel-grandes-écoles.com – hotel-grandes-écoles@wanadoo.fr

You'll be struck by the charm of the vast courtyard—flowered and peaceful—from the moment you set foot in the door of this somewhat outdated hotel, a sort of provincial enclave in the heart of the fifth arrondissement. With old-fashioned crocheted bedspreads and functional, comfortable bathrooms, the double room opening onto the garden offers simple and rare luxury. In nice weather, breakfast is served outside, making for a serene and luminous way to start the day. 530 to 690 francs (80,80–105,19 €).

6th arrondissement

HÔTEL D'ANGLETERRE / *Classic and sporty*
44, rue Jacob, 6th arr., M° Saint-Germain-des-Prés
Tel.: 01.42.60.34.72 – fax: 01.42.60.16.93

It is neither for its listed staircase, nor for the rooms' undefined style—most with sloped ceilings evoking the relaxed atmosphere of a ski chalet, fireplaces included—that we've listed this hotel, former seat of the British embassy…but rather for its genuine good value and the soothing southern spirit of its rectangular interior courtyard, with its promise of relaxation after long days of pounding the pavement. From 750 francs (114,34 €).

HÔTEL DU DANUBE / *Chintz and cane*
58, rue Jacob, 6th arr., M° Saint-Germain-des-Prés
Tel.: 01.42.60.34.70 – fax: 01.42.60.81.18

With lots of flowery fabric, and scattered Chinese porcelain, chintz, and cane furniture, this ornate and gracious little hotel is chock full of character. It's hard to explain why one succumbs to its charms: partly for its interior courtyard and spruce dining room, partly for its relaxed interior decor, but mostly for its neighborhood and reasonable range of prices. From 650 to 1150 francs (99,10–175,32 €).

HÔTEL DU GLOBE / *Cozy Left Bank*
15, rue des Quatre-Vents, 6th arr., M° Saint-Germain-des-Prés
Tel.: 01.43.26.35.50 – fax: 01.46.33.62.69
hotelglobe@post.club-internet.fr

Here is a little hotel without pretension but worthy of interest. Each one unique, the fifteen narrow rooms with their exposed beams and canopy beds have a cozy and rural charm. Remarkable for its reasonable prices in this strategic location in the heart of Saint-Germain, between Odéon and Saint-Sulpice. From around 400 to 600 francs (61–91,50 €).

L'HÔTEL / *Utterly unique*
13, rue des Beaux-Arts, 6th arr., M° Saint-Germain-des-Prés
Tel.: 01.43.25.27.22 – fax: 01.43.25.64.81
reservation@l-hotel.com

Formerly a six-story lovers' meeting place, l'Hôtel's only sober feature is its name. Beyond the reception area it's all quite extraordinary: the light well opening onto the sky around which all the rooms are situated like opera loges; the bar lit up by a stained-glass wall; the dominantly red color scheme of the sitting room where a tree grows beside a stone fountain, its trunk pushing through the paneled ceiling.... Strange, extravagant, half-Empire style, half-sixties, this little palace is a gem still haunted by the presence of Oscar Wilde (room #16, opening onto a flowering terrace overlooking the roofs) and by the celebrated music-hall star Mistinguett (room #36, Art Deco). During the high season, the prices vary from 1000 francs (152,45 €) for a single room to 4000 francs (609,80 €) for the apartment, and from 800 to 2500 francs off-season (122–381,12 €).

HÔTEL DES MARRONNIERS / *Bright and lovely*
21, rue Jacob, 6th arr., M° Saint-Germain-des-Prés
Tel. : 01.43.25.30.60 – fax : 01.40.46.83.56

On a sweltering hot summer afternoon, we happened upon the gravel courtyard of the Hôtel des Marronniers, open to thirsty passers-by. The serenity of the grounds, the shade, the daintily furnished veranda and sumptuous bouquets of flowers in the entrance all made us want to learn more about this oasis. Adorable, calm, well-kept rooms bathed in light. Two steps from the Café Flore, this is a real find. Count on 580 francs (88,42 €) for a single room with shower, and around 1000 francs (152,45 €) for a double room with bath.

7th arrondissement

APPT LIVING IN PARIS / *Group rentals*
47, avenue de Ségur, 7th arr., M° Ségur
Tel. : 01.45.67.27.90 – fax : 01.40.66.60.90
www.apartment-living.com – apartment.living@wanadoo.fr

If you plan to spend more than a few days and are with friends, why not rent a three, four, or five-room place together? High-end luxury apartments are available on the rue de Lille, rue du Faubourg-Saint-Honoré, and in the Monceau area for between 1000 and 3000 francs per day (152,45–457,35 €), depending on whether you rent by the week or the month.

HÔTEL MONTALEMBERT / *Designer bachelor pad*
3, rue de Montalembert, 7th arr., M° Rue-du-Bac
Tel. : 01.45.49.68.68 – fax : 01.45.49.69.49
www.montalembert.com – welcome@hotel-montalembert.fr

Decorated by Christian Liaigre (see p. 77), with refined sycamore furnishings, ebony paneling, wide-striped navy blue fabric, and floral arrangements of wildflowers and eucalyptus by Christian Tortu, the Montalembert—renovated in 1990—is one of the rare "designer" hotels in the capital. This specialty makes it one of the favorites of the fashion crowd, who has made it their meeting place of choice. The sophistication of the place, with its library/sitting room with fireplace and beige leather couches (that will remind you of those chic, muted, writers' bachelor pads featured in magazines), compensates for the modest size of the rooms. Rooms from 1750 to 2300 francs; suites between 2850 and 4400 francs (434,48–670,78 €).

LE TOURVILLE / *Family-style four-star*
16, avenue de Tourville, 7th arr., M° Saint-François-Xavier, École-militaire
Tel.: 01.47.05.62.62 – fax: 01.47.05.43.90
www.hoteltourville.com – hotel@tourville.com

In shades of buttercup, pink, and pale apricot, the rooms in this four-star hotel exude an aura of peace and simplicity. We particularly recommend the small apartments located on the top floor—junior suites equipped with large bathrooms and fanlights (1990 francs or 303,37 €). Equally appealing are the two rooms at 1390 francs (211,90 €) that open onto private terraces spacious enough for a breakfast table and two chaise lounges in the midst of potted plants.

8th arrondissement

HÔTEL BRISTOL / *Beyond perfect*
112, rue du Faubourg-Saint-Honoré, 8th arr., M° Saint-Philippe-du-Roule
Tel.: 01.53.43.43.00 – fax: 01.53.43.43.01
www.hotel/bristol.com – resa@hotel/bristol.com

Of all the hotels in the capital, the Bristol is certainly the most superlative. The decoration of the rooms, each unique and for the most part renovated from scratch, recreates the most classical and perfect bourgeois tradition of comfort. Even if you aren't one to notice the period-style renovation, the splendor (Carrara marble bathrooms, a spectacular entrance hall) attains grandiose proportions here. Room service is available 24 hours a day—whether you'd like your laundry done or want to dine at 5 A.M. To enjoy the class of the Bristol even if you don't choose to stay here, note that the marvelous garden is open all summer—ideal for ice cream or a slice of tart—and that a pianist plays in the bar around 8 P.M. each evening. From 2950 francs (449,72 €).

Chapter 1

HÔTEL LANCASTER / *Discreetly luxurious*
7, rue de Berri, 8th arr., M° George-V
Tel.: 01.40.76.40.76 – fax : 01.40.76.40.00
www.hotel-lancaster.fr

For three years Marlene Dietrich inhabited one of the sixty rooms of the Lancaster, renovated in 1996. Why would the diva cast her fate with this elegant palace? Perhaps, if it existed at that time, for its interior garden decorated in the spirit of Balinese spas, where the Zen and exotic atmosphere offers an appealing touch of modernity. Undoubtedly for its marvelous little dollhouse sitting rooms where one wants to pull the door shut after entering, and surely for the discretion of the place, so close and yet so far from the Champs-Élysées. From 1950 francs (297,28 €).

LE LAVOISIER / *Contemporary spirit*
21, rue Lavoisier, 8th arr., M° Saint-Augustin
Tel.: 01.53.30.06.06 – fax : 01.53.30.23.00
info@hotellavoisier.com

Just a few steps from the place de la Madeleine and the faubourg Saint-Honoré, the recently renovated Le Lavoisier is one of those places we'd like to keep under wraps. At affordable rates given its location, this hotel is appealing for its modern yet warm atmosphere. The tone is set at the entrance, closer to the sitting room than the reception desk, and continues in the light-filled rooms, elegantly furnished with soft colors, pure lines, and thick carpeting—and as an added plus, most are equipped with a Jacuzzi. The breakfast room, located under ocher-colored arches, clinches our admiration for this intimate and cozy spot, already discovered and taken over by Prada's staff and the editors of Italian Vogue during last season's fashion shows. From 890 francs (135,68 €).

16th arrondissement
HÔTEL RAPHAËL / *Seventh heaven*
17, avenue Kléber, 16th arr., M° Kléber
Tel.: 01.44.28.00.28 – fax : 01.45.01.21.50
www.raphael-hotel.com – management@raphael-hotel.com

A muted atmosphere steeped in oak and walnut wood, Aubusson tapestries, canvas-backed fabrics, and Louis XVI furnishings. The Raphaël magnificently illustrates the idea of unsurpassable French taste. Curiously Left Bank in spirit, the Raphaël is simply one of those places to see and in which to be seen. If you choose not to stay here, indulge in a bit of seventh heaven with breakfast, lunch, or a drink on one of the top floor terraces. Planted with lavender and rosemary hanging above a panoramic view of the city, this spot is utterly unique. From 2350 francs (358,26 €).

ST. JAMES PARIS / *British touch*
43, avenue Bugeaud, 16th arr., M° Porte-Dauphine
Tel. : 01.44.05.81.81 – fax : 01.53.65.66.88

Formerly the Thiers foundation, later a club with British overtones, and finally transformed in the nineties into the most exclusive of all Parisian establishments, this neo-classical castle/hotel has the appeal of an old patrician home. Located between the Champs-Élysées and La Défense, it has obviously found favor with businessmen who enjoy most of all its insiders' atmosphere—the restaurant, bar, and gym are all reserved exclusively for hotel guests. An unexpected fantasyland beyond the somewhat austere entrance hall, with a "Chesterfield and blond tobacco" atmosphere in the superb wood-paneled bar/library, the rooms on the top floor hold the real surprise. Decorated by Andrée Putman, they open onto a winter garden composed of private terraces and illuminated by natural light. From 1850 francs (282 €).

TROCADÉRO DOKHAN'S / *Intimate*
117, rue Lauriston, 16th arr., M° Boissière, Trocadéro
Tel. : 01.53.65.66.99
hotel.trocadero.dokhans@wanadoo.fr

A few steps from the Trocadéro, Dokhan's is the hotel that people are talking about these days. The spirit of a private residence cultivated by interior designer Frédéric Méchiche is appealing from the moment you step inside the entry hall—small, round, and tiled in a black-and-white-marble checkered pattern. From the eighteenth-century living room gilded with gold leaf to the intimate blue, mauve, and beige-striped bedrooms with mahogany hues and hand-sewn details (moiré silk curtains cover the heaters), the effect can—depending who you are—exasperate or enrapture. But coming out of the Louis-Vuitton-monogrammed elevator to have a glass of champagne at the candlelit bar is an experience not lacking in charm. From 1900 francs (289,65 €).

TABLES

Tables]

Paris is definitely still the food capital of the
world. Every kind of culinary experience is
available, be it premeditated or last minute—from indulging
your wildest gastronomic fantasies to simply avoiding an empty
fridge. As a result, every personality, every desire, and every mood
has its restaurant—and each Parisian his secret addresses. Eating
out in Paris can be likened to a lovely and inexhaustible treasure
hunt. Yes, it is possible to feast for under 100 francs (15,24 €); we
will tell you where. But we especially want you to satisfy your appetite in places full of character, charm, and history. It's this perfect
mix of "form and content" that guided our selection.

1st arrondissement

L'ARDOISE / *Business lunches*
28, rue du Mont-Thabor, 1st arr., M° Concorde
Tel.: 01.42.96.28.18 ▪ **Closed Saturdays for lunch and Mondays** ▪

Located near the place Vendôme, Pierre Jay's fixed-price lunch menu is a god-send for the neighborhood. There's nothing spectacular about the setting (that's the least that can be said), but the meal itself—that we'd rather savor for lunch given the absence of decorum—is good value. Crab with basil, magnificent *langoustines* (small lobsters) with mayonnaise, sauté of veal with salsify—it's classic and impeccable, with prices in the range of 145 to 170 francs (22,10–25,92 €).

AU BISTRO / *Traditional French fare*
8, rue du Marché-Saint-Honoré, 1st arr., M° Tuileries
Tel.: 01.42.61.02.45 ▪ **Closed evenings and Sundays** ▪

Although only a few dozen yards from Colette (see p. 80), the temple of trendiness, Au Bistro is separated by light years in spirit. Passing from the hipness of the former to the checkered tablecloths of the latter is a bit like inviting yourself to your aunt's in the country for just a quick bite, knowing that you will always be warmly received, but that she will inevitably find you a bit pale. Welcomed by the owner Evelyne, you certainly won't snub her aromatic and juicy stuffed tomatoes, invigorating *pot-au-feu,* or her creamy blanquette—by-the-book bourgeois cuisine that you can accompany with a choice from over fifteen wines sold by the glass. Count on about 150 francs (22,87 €).

IL CORTILE / *Italian skies*
37, rue Cambon, 1st arr., M° Concorde
Tel.: 01.44.58.45.67 ▪ **Closed Saturdays and Sundays** ▪

Although in the heart of winter we appreciate the stylish service, opulent and contemporary furnishings, refined table linens, and the variations on an Italian menu revisited by Alain Ducasse, we especially love to frequent this very stylish hotel restaurant for lunch come summer. The reason is simple: Il Cortile has, as the name indicates, a dream patio. If a bit chilled inside be-tween the pale lemon yellow walls, the food finds its colors and aromas—citrus zest, balsamic vinegar—as soon as it's consumed under the open sky, rocked by the continual murmur of the fountain. It's no surprise to see Karl Lagerfeld in the shade of the great white canvas parasols, as the designer often reserves a table here. Count on 250 francs (38,11 €).

CHEZ DENISE / *All night long*
5, rue des Prouvaires, 1st arr., M° Les Halles
Tel. : 01.42.36.21.82 ▪ Closed Saturdays and Sundays ▪

Open round-the-clock, this bistro in the area of Les Halles serves a robust cuisine (mutton stew, ham hock with lentils) in a post-party atmosphere. Between shapeless benches and old barrels, with the constant hum of laughter and wedding banquet toasts, this place is clearly for only the most advanced hours of the night. Count on 250 francs (38,11 €).

HIGUMA / *Japanese noodles*
32 *bis*, rue Sainte-Anne, 1st arr., M° Pyramides
Tel. : 01.47.03.38.59

There is Zen Japan with its refined sophistication, and there is the people's Japan with its rural roots. It's the second that you'll find when you pass through the door of this noodle house. With vast neon-lit cafeteria-style rooms bubbling with the lively chatter of the more or less illustrious clients, it's best to grab a seat at the bar to behold the fascinating spectacle of sizzling woks, where four cooks work nonstop with precise and impeccable maneuvers. In a clear broth, they'll mix the ingredients—vegetables, meats, noodles, or fish—depending on your selection among the twenty soups under 50 francs (7,62 €) that constitute the basis for the menu. The boiled noodles barely tossed in oil are delicious. Here, more than in any other Japanese restaurant, it's best to order your sake lukewarm, because the rice wine—as basic and efficient as the food it accompanies—will be served in a Pyrex glass full to the brim.

JOE ALLEN / *All-comfort ranch*
30, rue Pierre-Lescot, 1st arr., M° Étienne-Marcel
Tel. : 01.42.36.70.13

We take refuge here in winter; come summer, we perch on high bar stools, basking on the terrace, far from the droning of the traffic. On Sundays for its copious brunch; during the week because—wanting neither Chinese, nor Italian, nor Thai, nor...—the prospect of an excellent tuna steak and enormous salad or a good grilled steak is a delightful thought. You don't go to Joe Allen's to be surprised, but for the very comfort of never being so. The casual ranch-style setting, the pleasant staff, the pot of butter for the thick slices of bread, the efficiency of the service—everything contributes to the simple pleasure of settling down here for a satisfying meal. About 250 francs (38,11 €).

TAISHIN / *Sushi bar*
2, rue du Mont-Thabor, 1st arr., M° Concorde
Tel.: 01.42.96.44.78

The restaurant in the Monthabor hotel is run independently, and is a pleasing option for a hotel restaurant. At noon, the *Bento Taishin* platter (raw salmon and tuna, crayfish and vegetable tempura, grilled mackerel, assorted carrots, turnips, mushrooms, and a bit of sticky rice) is divinely satisfying. It's consumed at the bar, on comfortable seats overlooking the shrimp, octopuses, and calamar glistening behind glass, and facing the cook busy with his meticulous preparations. Sheltered by dark wood blinds, the setting is reminiscent of restaurants in the business district of Tokyo—and somewhat less frenetic. A strategic stop between Colette and Maria Luiso (see pp. 80 and 82). About 100 francs (15,24 €).

2nd arrondissement

CHEZ GEORGES / *Authentic brasserie*
1, rue du Mail, 2nd arr., M° Bourse
Tel.: 01.42.60.07.11 ▪ Closed Sundays ▪

The only unknown in a dinner at Chez Georges is the matter of finding a free table if you haven't thought to reserve one ahead of time. Always packed, this old-style brasserie, with its tinted glass and period-style moldings, has such authentic charm that Parisians regularly invite their American colleagues or provincial cousins here. You're sure never to be surprised here: from the cold lentil salad served directly from the salad bowl to the whole grilled turbot served with béarnaise sauce, kidneys cooked to perfection, and grilled mushrooms, everything is exquisite. The maternal waitresses add to the good-natured spirit of the place. Unfortunately, it's fairly pricey—about 300 francs (45,73 €).

ISSÉ / *Tokyo chic*
56, rue Sainte-Anne, 2nd arr., M° Pyramides, Quatre-Septembre
Tel.: 01.42.96.67.76 ▪ Closed Sundays ▪

With its luminous woodwork and lighting, Zen and muted atmosphere, and delicate interior, Issé—formerly the Kenzo cafeteria—remains one of the most chic Japanese restaurants in the neighborhood. A detail we appreciate: the place basks in amber light auspicious for secrets and relaxation. Tempura cooked according to your wishes, very fresh sushi—Japanese cuisine at its best. 350 francs (53,36 €).

Chapter 2

JUVENILE'S / *Cosmopolitan wine bar*
47, rue de Richelieu, 2nd arr., M° Pyramides
Tel.: 01.42.97.46.49 ▪ Closed Sundays ▪

What's in a setting.... That of Juvenile's, when you enter midweek, seems white-hot. It's a place to laugh out loud and chat raucously, encouraged by the discovery of a good bottle of wine from Australia or Spain and accompanied by grilled squid, eggplant tapenade, and a meat or fish dish. The seagull hanging from a string, the innocent drawings on the wall, and the camping tables summarize the casual philosophy of this wine bar owned by a truculent Scotsman: please leave all serious matters at the door. About 200 francs (30,49 €).

3rd arrondissement

L'AMI LOUIS / *Fit for a king*
32, rue du Vert-Bois, 3rd arr., M° Arts-et-Métiers
Tel.: 01.48.87.77.48 ▪ Closed Mondays and Tuesdays ▪

You'll find a posh clientele at this Parisian institution that can certainly afford it given the prices. Every last one of them is willing to good-naturedly recognize that the white-glove service is not always affable and the tab is exorbitant, but nevertheless happy to continue to frequent this high ground of Parisian snobbery for the pleasure of being able to do so. Only left to mention is the roast chicken and potatoes, the game, and the wild strawberries said to be the best in the world, consumed in copious portions in a wooden bowl. About 500 francs (76,22 €).

ANAHI / *Fashionable grill*
49, rue Volta, 3rd arr., M° Arts-et-Métiers
Tel.: 01.48.87.88.24

You might look for this place for a good while before stopping in front of the mildew-tinted windows decorated with high branches of nut trees and potted cactuses. You enter this meat shop with its tiled walls as though into another dimension. The place is haunted, certainly, but by a well-meaning ghost. It could be somewhere in Havana; it certainly doesn't resemble any other place. The guacamole is unique, as are the marvelously spicy *ceviche* (bass marinated in lime with coriander) and the grills that would make even a hardened vegetarian succumb because the meat is so flavorful. You'll need to have enough appetite left to revel in the moist *empanadas*, corn gratin, chorizo, and candied oranges with ginger and milk candies. And to boot, you must quench your thirst with *caipirina*, daikiri, *mojito*, or wine from Riojo. Patrice Chereau, old acquaintance of Carmina and Pilar, has his seat here.

Regulars have already run into Naomi Campbell, John Galliano, Tom Ford, and Armani, and know that late at night the tables are sometimes pushed back to make room for flamenco dancing. To be avoided at all costs during fashion week. To be visited regularly all other days of the year. About 250 francs (38,11 €).

LE 404 / *Trendy couscous*
69, rue des Gravilliers, 3rd arr., M° Arts-et-Métiers
Tel.: 01.42.74.57.81

Located in a very old private mansion, Le 404 happily cultivates a family and Oriental setting. The excellent *tajines* (slow-baked dishes) are inventive (on Sundays, don't miss the delicious "Berber brunch" with a base of sweet grain) and will convince the most finicky enthusiasts of Moroccan cuisine. To take full advantage of the place, reserve the only table on the mezzanine: you'll dine there on cushions, taking yourself for Scheherazade. About 250 francs (38,11 €).

4th arrondissement

L'AMBROISIE / *Pure extravagance*
9, place des Vosges, 4th arr., M° Saint-Paul
Tel.: 01.42.78.51.45 ▪ Closed Sundays and Mondays ▪

A three-star restaurant unlike any other—no ostentatious pomp in this pretty house bordering the place des Vosges. Three sitting rooms in a row hold forty places, with a rare spacious luxury. The space is devoted to the simple ballet of the staff, the indirect lighting of the crystal fixtures, the discreet wall lamps, the large mirrors, the rich tapestries, the heavy drapes at the windows—everything contributes to the quiet and serene climate of the place. Each of the rooms has its own personality. On a vast table of game, an intentionally casual assortment of objects—pottery, crystal decanters, cigar cases, sumptuous bouquets of flowers—are composed like a still life in the seventeenth-century-style first room. The second, bigger in size, links old rose and golden-bronze tones, in a sort of homage to a faded Versailles. The third, in nineteenth-century style, has the mood of an intimate Chinese cabinet where you can seat yourself apart in a small committee. The sobriety of the silverware, the Sèvres crystal glasses, and the small silver bowls garnished with miniature roses are all in harmony with a cuisine that seeks to bring out the best in the ingredients. Bernard Pacau supervises the kitchen but never ventures into the dining rooms, where everyone is treated with the same regard, whether it be groups of refined gourmets or the Chiracs dining with Bill and Hillary Clinton.

BOFINGER / *Seafood and theatrical setting*
5, rue de la Bastille, 4th arr., M° Bastille
Tel.: 01.42.72.87.82

From the height of its paneled dining rooms, one hundred and thirty years of history look down on you. And that's the real significance of this historically preserved brasserie. If, when coming out of the opera at the Bastille, you are in the mood for a thematic evening, prolong it in this breathtaking theatrical decor. With its masterpieces and inlaid mosaics, everything is sumptuous, from the rooms upstairs to the bathrooms in the basement. Bofinger is a place to keep in mind for spectacular seafood platters. About 250 francs (38,11 €).

DANE GOURMANDE / *Tasty dishes*
9, rue de Turenne, 4th arr., M° Saint-Paul
Tel.: 01.42.77.62.54 ▪ Closed Mondays for lunch ▪

This Alsatian septuagenarian left the rue du Cherche-Midi but decided not to abandon the stove. Place settings for up to a dozen people fit into what resembles a well-run family boarding house. Dane works alone in the kitchen and dining room—and works wonders. At lunchtime, the 110-franc (16,80 €) fixed menu includes a first course (five-pepper duck terrine, mild Spanish-style anchovies), a main course (pheasant thigh, Indian-style stuffed eggplant, free-range chicken with Alsatian sparkling wine), dessert (lemon tart, *crème caramel*), and a half-bottle of Bordeaux! Nothing is heavy, dry, or overcooked. The pleasure stems as much from watching this ample cook fret lovingly over her simmering dishes as from her understanding of spices acquired during trips to the far ends of the earth. You'll feel pampered and happy. 110 francs for lunch (16,80 €), 250 francs a la carte (38,11 €).

L'ENOTECA / *Pasta after the opera*
25, rue Charles-V, 4th arr., M° Saint-Paul
Tel.: 01.42.78.91.44

In a surprisingly calm part of the Marais, this Italian gem is the place to go for a "post-Bastille" meal, praying that there will be a free table if you haven't reserved one. On the first floor, which we prefer to the upstairs, exposed beams and floor tiles warm up the cheerful room—laid out in such a way that you won't dine elbow-to-elbow with your neighbors. An exquisite and astonishing transalpine wine menu, tagliatelle with cuttlefish ink, mushroom risotto, delicious stuffed ravioli—a short menu perfect for evenings when you're craving a simple bowl of pasta and an excellent bottle of red wine. About 250 francs (38,11 €).

ISAMI / *Zen snacks*
4, quai d'Orléans, 4th arr., M° Saint-Paul
Tel. : 01.40.46.06.97 ▪ **Closed Sundays for lunch and Mondays** ▪

We let ourselves be convinced that the *makis* (sushi rolls) in this discreetly trendy Japanese restaurant were worth the detour by the Île Saint-Louis. The prospect of a stroll along the river bank in the mild evening air made the discovery all the more appealing. Nothing disappointing about the excellent incredibly fresh fish or the elegant clientele. Our only regret in retrospect: the lack of warmth in the place, from which we emerged feeling that this delicious but frugal nibble had been merely enough to whet our appetites. For small stomachs only. About 200 francs (30,49 €).

L'OSTÉRIA / *Venetian inspiration*
10, rue de Sévigné, 4th arr., M° Saint-Paul
Tel. : 01.42.71.37.08 ▪ **Closed Saturdays and Sundays** ▪

Loyal to his poultry man from Landes, the Venetian chef of l'Osteria can move you by the simple creation of his squab in Armagnac or his foie gras. His creamy risotto is voluptuous; his *osso buco a la gremolata* (oxtail sprinkled with lemon zest), veal stew, and cod blanquette with rice batter all utterly delicious. This little Italian restaurant is actually known to be the favorite headquarters of Sony Music in the place des Vosges. Discreet, but therefore hip. About 250 francs (38,11 €).

5th arrondissement

BALZAR / *Historical brasserie*
49, rue des Écoles, 5th arr., M° Cluny-La-Sorbonne
Tel. : 01.43.54.13.67

When the owners of the Flo chain took over this hundred-year-old-plus brasserie, the faithful of Balzar united and threatened them with heavy reprisals at the first sign of change. Nothing has moved: in an intact 1930s decor, you eat succulent meat or skate with melted butter, perfect fries, and divinely warm apple tart elbow-to-elbow between two Sorbonne professors and some journalists. Perfect for frivolous and famished evenings after the theater. We do not recommend it for romantic dinners for two, as you'll be packed in pretty tightly in this warm and bustling setting.

Chapter 2

CHIENG MAÏ / *Flavors of Thailand*
12, rue Frédéric-Sauton, 5th arr., M° Maubert-Mutualité
Tel.: 01.43.25.45.45

Lovers of Thai food sing the praises of this restaurant that's remained unchanged for twenty years. Chieng Mai is appealing for its simple food (five-flavor monkfish, fish cooked in banana leaves) and the extreme kindness of the owner. Perfect for a small gathering of friends without having to spend a fortune. About 150 francs (22,87 €).

AU COIN DES GOURMETS / *Southeast Asian delicacies*
5, rue Dante, 5th arr., M° Maubert-Mutualité
Tel.: 01.43.26.12.92

Neither the name nor the decor of this tidy Indo-Chinese restaurant hidden behind its old-fashioned curtains would seem to be an invitation to the exotic. Yet we'd be hard-pressed to find anything more succulent than their fish with coconut milk cooked in banana leaves, more aromatic than the tamarind and duck soup, crispier than the golden Saigonese crepe—baked with bean sprouts, pork, shrimp, and served on a sparkling, fresh bed of mint and lettuce. The address of this family-style Cambodian place, where you can have a great time at a reasonable price, is nevertheless known to traveling Parisians nostalgic for Asian cuisine. During the summer, the sidewalk terrace invites you to prolong your light but satisfying meal.

MIRAMA / *Trendy Chinese*
15, rue Saint-Jacques, 5th arr., M° Maubert-Mutualité
Tel.: 01.43.54.71.77

From the street, behind windows misted over by the kitchen set up in the entryway, you can imagine the haphazard look of the vast dining rooms crammed with people. You'll stop in front of a menu offering a selection of close to two hundred dishes, and you'll enter with good reason into what is undoubtedly one of the least expensive and most delicious Chinese restaurants in the city. The European and Asian clientele is a mix of young couples and families; you'll occasionally run into a few celebrities in the know who've come to eat on the spot (but more often to discreetly pick up take-out). Noodles in oyster sauce, shrimp with black beans, beef with spicy vegetables, and steamed duck—all of it served in generous portions and all the better washed down with a cold Tsingtao beer. About 150 francs (22,87 €).

6th arrondissement

DA ALFREDO POSITANO / *Mouth-watering trattoria*
9, rue Guisarde, 6th arr., M° Mabillon
Tel.: 01.43.26.90.52 ▪ Closed Sundays ▪

This highly-recommended trattoria—long, narrow, always full and cheer-ful—has the unusual practice of spreading out its market goods for all to see: lettuces in their crate, shellfish, sea bream (*dorade*), bass, mushrooms, and various *antipasti* compose a colorful and mouth-watering tableau. All the great classics of Italian cuisine are here, from octopus salad to *tagliatelli a la carbonara*. The pizzas are excellent, which, paradoxically, is not always the case in an Italian restaurant. About 200 francs (30,49 €).

LA BASTIDE ODÉON / *Sophisticated Provence*
2, rue Corneille, 6th arr., M° Odéon
Tel.: 01.43.26.03.65 ▪ Closed Sundays and Mondays ▪

The atmosphere here resembles that of a large bourgeois home—ideal for evenings at the theater (the Odéon is just a few steps away) or the movies. With its attractive, somewhat precious decor, inventive Provençal cuisine (eggplant-filled *mille-feuilles*, tuna with veal juices, cinnamon *crème brûlée*), and attentive service, it's easy to disregard the slightly stuffy clientele, which is more mixed at the second seating. About 250 francs (38,11 €).

CASA BINI / *A breath of fresh air*
36, rue Grégoire-de-Tours, 6th arr., M° Saint-Germain-des-Prés
Tel.: 01.46.34.05.60 ▪ Closed Sundays for lunch ▪

Casa Bini is first and foremost a family story: Anna Bini passed the restau-rant down to her son Simon, who dutifully left his grandmother's original Tuscan recipes on the menu—as they had assured the success of the place in its early days. Bass carpaccio with oregano, beef with grilled vegetables, seafood pasta with orange or lemon, ham or cuttlefish ink *crostini*.... The wood, stone, and Siennese terracotta interior, along with the olive tree, give this place a sunny atmosphere; you're always running into well-known faces and other Left Bank regulars. About 250 francs (38,11 €).

Chapter 2

LE CHERCHE-MIDI / *La dolce vita*
22, rue du Cherche-Midi, 6th arr., M° Sèvres-Babylone
Tel.: 01.45.48.27.44

Promoted less than a year ago to head of the dining room and kitchen, Franco restructured the team at this cheerful Italian place, convinced that the misunderstandings between the French waiters and the kitchen staff weren't doing justice to the menu. From now on, Matteo and Remo inform you of the fresh market arrivals in their Peninsula accent. You will no longer hesitate among twenty dishes, but choose between ten daily specials that combine standard ingredients imported from Italy with daily market finds, such as *cigales de mer* (crayfish-like rock lobster) and other curious surprises. After having shared a plate of *antipasti* worthy of the best trattorias (crisp white beans, eggplant, and peppers that melt on the tongue, fresh spinach tossed with a trickle of olive oil, thin slices of omelette with baby vegetables) and opting for the big *raviolis al dente* covered in an aromatic tomato sauce and sprinkled with parmesan, we capitulated and abandoned any thought of the house dessert. Wrapping up instead with a cup of coffee and a glass of *lemone*, we emerged into the gray winter's day, mellowed by a perfect meal and a diffuse nostalgia for the dolce vita summoned by the decor of this Parisian bistro. About 200 francs (30,49 €).

CLAUDE SAINT-LOUIS / *The ultimate steak and fries*
27, rue du Dragon, 6th arr., M° Saint-Germain-des-Prés
Tel.: 01.45.44.62.83

The best fries in Paris are consumed on a backdrop of blood-red moleskin benches and dark floral tapestries. A funny place that's something of a cross between a saloon and a provincial pub, Claude Saint-Louis is an institution full of charm—deserted when you walk in, but then suddenly packed with a flow of regulars just when you're finishing up. With friendly service, this place has a cheerful soul and lots of integrity. About 200 francs (30,49 €).

OKU / *Nicely priced sashimi*
48, rue Grégoire-de-Tours, 6th arr., M° Saint-Germain-des-Prés
Tel.: 01.43.25.41.86

It's useless to look for Oku in the phone book, because you won't find it.... And if you ask the owner for the phone number, she will give you instead, in the guise of a business card, beautiful origami flowers that you will want to save preciously. In the heart of Saint-Germain-des-Prés, this family-style Japanese restaurant with its white wood furniture is providential: at lunchtime, the menu costs between 50 and 70 francs (7,62–10,67 €). It's not unusual to be offered Japanese-style grilled oysters, cuttlefish, sea urchin, or prune puree—as well as excellent sashimi, sushi, and tempura. This is the time to try that famous traditional dessert, *okan*, a disconcertingly exotic sweet made with red beans.

7th arrondissement

AU PIED DE FOUET / *Gourmet hangout*
45, rue de Babylone, 7th arr., M° Vaneau
Tel.: 01.47.05.12.27 ▪ Closed Saturday evenings and Sundays ▪

This minuscule two-story tavern decorated with crocheted tablecloths and checkered fabrics is a former stagecoach rest stop. A lair for refined palates (regulars have their own napkin holders), it offers the opportunity to enjoy a lentil salad or house foie gras, steak and puree or sautéed chicken livers, and chestnut cream or pudding for dessert. It's so typically French you'll want to pinch yourself to make sure it's real. Around 80 francs (12,20 €).

8th arrondissement

BAR DES THÉÂTRES / *All-Parisian*
6, avenue Montaigne, 8th arr., M° Alma-Marceau
Tel.: 01.47.23.34.63

As the Théâtre des Champs-Élysées lets out, the crowd generally divides in two: one column heads in the direction of Le Relais Plaza (see p. 31), while the other sweeps into the Bar des Théâtres along with the orchestra. This old café will throw you for a loop with its illustrious past—its clientele of old ladies dressed to the nines and trendy couples, a mix of past glory and a young Parisian glow. When they're not on the attack, the waiters are of a rare affability; we can only suggest that you do as everyone else does and order a steak tartare with salad and fries. About 200 francs (30,49 €).

GARNIER / *Shellfish and crustaceans*
11, rue Saint-Lazare, 8th arr., M° Saint-Lazare
Tel.: 01.43.87.50.40

Even without the top-quality seafood, we would undoubtedly come here simply to take in the staggering kitsch museum. It's better not to let yourself be taken in by the sight of the sad-looking sixties dining room; instead turn your back on it altogether by taking a seat at the bar facing the Saint-Lazare train station. Always extremely fresh, the shellfish, fish, and crustaceans are all worth the trip. About 200 francs (30,49 €).

LA MAISON BLANCHE / *Business with a view*
15, avenue Montaigne, 8th arr., M° Alma-Marceau
Tel. : 01.47.23.55.99 ▪ Closed Saturdays and Mondays for lunch and Sundays ▪

On the roof of the Théâtre des Champs-Élysées, you would think you were on top of the world: the show biz and business crowds mix with the fashion milieu with a spectacular panoramic view as a backdrop. The flowery garden is lovely, the perspective exquisite, the decor very "New York, New York," the conversations hyper-secretive, and the cuisine—perhaps most importantly—refined. Very pricey, so chic.... About 800 francs (121,96 €).

PIERRE GAGNAIRE / *Culinary genius*
6, rue de Balzac, 8th arr., M° George-V
Tel. : 01.44.35.18.25 ▪ Closed Saturdays and Sundays ▪

Pierre Gagnaire speaks of cooking as though it were poetry, and understandably: you will witness a demonstration of culinary genius at his place. "Pressed crab, calfskin and white tuna belly with chanterelle mushrooms from Corrèze and baby leeks; bouquets of 'deer horn' (plantain leaves) with *mizuna* and Cramone mustard; John Dory pierced with capers and seared in herb butter; tandoori of shoots and cuttlefish with whole shallots; caramelized shrimp in broth; gnocchi with thistle"—the menu must be deciphered like a musical score and the most lyrical of its fans will tell you that an evening at Gagnaire's is worth a top loge at the opera. With blue and pale gray stripes and elm-wood paneling, it is impossible to be disappointed here and difficult not to be astonished by this chef who seeks to surprise even himself on a daily basis. A real and true pleasure for two; an unforgettable folly. About 900 francs (137,20 €).

LE RELAIS PLAZA / *Second sitting*
21, avenue Montaigne, 8th arr., M° Alma-Marceau
Tel. : 01.53.67.64.00

You must reserve a table at Le Relais Plaza for after the theater, when the patrons look like they've surfaced from another era, another world. The atmosphere in this thirties steamship decor is utterly unique, all beige tones lit by apricot highlights in the silk curtains. Between an orchestra conductor and a soprano, you can indulge in fried scampi with tartar sauce, a club sandwich, or a steak with matchstick French fries—knowing that if the boat were to sink, you would have made the most of your life until the very end. About 350 francs (53,36 €).

SPOON FOOD AND WINE / *Interactive menu*
14, rue de Marignan, 8th arr., M° Franklin-Roosevelt
Tel.: 01.40.76.36.66 ▪ Closed Saturdays and Sundays ▪

When Alain Ducasse is happy, so are we. Opened in December 1998, this restaurant is without a doubt one of the most interesting places in town. Lined with wine-colored fabric, sprinkled with exotic wood, and lightened with pastel touches, the setting is simultaneously theatrical and intimate, so you'll feel a bit like you're comfortably ensconced in a theater loge (the little booths around the edges of the dining room are perfect for a tête-à-tête). It's your play though, with a menu that allows you to combine one of five kinds of meat or fish with the sauce and accompaniment of your choice. (More than two-thirds of the clientele doesn't venture beyond the suggested menu.) Titillated by this interactive game and the cosmopolitan quality of the dishes, we concocted our dinner among the dozens of possible combinations and were very, very pleased with our gastronomic audacity. We'd never had such culinary talent. The ultimate snobbery: amid its hundreds of references, the wine cellar holds only ten or so French labels—50% American wines, 40% wines of the world. About 350 francs (53,36 €).

9th arrondissement

WALLY LE SAHARIEN / *A thousand and one nights*
36, rue Rodier, 9th arr., M° Anvers
Tel.: 01.42.85.51.90 ▪ Closed Mondays for lunch and Sundays ▪

Moucharabieh, benches and cushions, muted lighting: the "Berber tent" atmosphere adds a great deal to the charm of this intimate place. As for the rest, Wally makes one of the best couscous in Paris. You won't choose from a menu here—you settle in comfortably and you eat. One, two, three courses proceed the main dish—powder-fine grains of couscous and succulent barbecued lamb—followed by an assortment of marvelous Oriental pastries. Beware though, this Saharan evening is not given away—but it's absolutely worth it. About 300 francs (45,73 €).

10th arrondissement

ANTOINE ET LILI / *World cuisine*
95, quai de Valmy, 10th arr., M° République
Tel.: 01.40.37.41.55

Let's be honest: Antoine and Lili's tearoom has not seen the light of day as we finish this guide, but the announcement of its opening is already something of a Parisian event. Behind the pink and green facade, various backdrops are being assembled: a Spanish bodega for tapas, Moroccan sitting room for sipping mint tea, Greek deli, and French grocery store. And there's more: you'll be able to buy garden and interior furniture in the midst of the plants. Nobody doubts that this "world" cafeteria will become the hot spot of the season. About 150 francs (22,87 €).

CHEZ CASIMIR / *Nifty neo-bistro*
6, rue de Belzunce, 10th arr., M° Gare-du-Nord, Poissonnière
Tel.: 01.48.78.28.80 ▪ Closed Saturdays for lunch and Sundays ▪

Well away from the beaten track, sheltered by the side of Saint-Vincent-de-Paul church, Casimir and Michel share a strangely calm location, a concern for authenticity, and a common bank account. As for the rest, it's impossible to confuse the two, even though we like them both. At Casimir's, in an interior reminiscent of a bistro set in a village opera (stone floor, waxed wood paneling, bouquets of dried flowers), you'll select a three-course menu at 125 francs (19,06 €) among the four listed on the chalkboard that will reflect the groceries purchased that day. It's not unusual for the French Southwest-inspired dishes to vary from morning to evening, since the chef has such a healthy and moral horror of freezing anything and makes his purchases in small quantities. When we were there, the fine semolina and olive codling and the made-to-order guinea fowl shepherd's pie were genuinely delightful. On the other hand, we had forgotten once again that Casimir doesn't take credit cards....

CHEZ MICHEL / *The pleasures of Brittany*
10, rue de Belzunce, 10th arr., M° Gare-du-Nord, Poissonnière
Tel.: 01.44.53.06.20 ▪ Closed Sundays and Mondays ▪

Dark exposed beams, wine-colored benches, and pale pink tablecloths set the tone of this discreet and classic inn. The rue de Belzunce isn't really a strolling street, but Michel always manages to fill his dining room. Neighborhood regulars and connoisseurs know that Thierry Breton is in charge and holds his own intelligently with inventive and reasonably priced cuisine. For something new and different, surprise friends with this excellent value, and spend a pleasant evening in this cozy place. Goat and artichoke lasagna, thyme-flavored thick-cut lamb *(pavé d'agneau), kouign amann* (an excellent cake from Brittany) for dessert.... A real pleasure for 180 francs (27,44 €).

CHEZ PRUNE / *On the canal*
36, rue de Beaurepaire, 10th arr., M° République
Tel.: 01.42.41.30.47

Here's proof that a small café can be both tidy and hip. The mix of furniture (bistro benches and cane armchairs) and clientele (half business, half teenagers) works well in this remodeled former bar/smoke shop, and benefits from a lovely terrace by the canal. There are vegetarian options at lunchtime, and in the evenings you can nibble at a plate of cold meats and salami *(charcuterie)*—a suitably simple cuisine in this infinitely relaxing environment. A real escape. About 100 francs (15,24 €).

11th arrondissement

ASTIER / *Straight up*
44, rue Jean-Pierre-Timbaud, 11th arr., M° Parmentier
Tel.: 01.43.57.16.35 ▪ Closed Saturdays and Sundays ▪

Old-fashioned curtains and simple furniture—you'll think you've stepped into the old country when you open the door to this bistro whose reputation has leaked well beyond the borders of the neighborhood. Always packed, Astier offers no-frills cuisine: house terrine, rabbit in mustard sauce, potato gratin, warm fig pockets with honey. For 140 francs (21,34 €), you'll savor the honest pleasure and comfort of wolfing down a full plate. Don't pass up the cheese platter—it's exceptional.

CHARDENOUX / *Historic building*
1, rue Jules-Vallès, 11th arr., M° Faidherbe
Tel.: 01.43.71.49.52 ▪ Closed Saturdays for lunch and Sundays ▪

It should come as no surprise that Hitchcock and Losey filmed certain scenes for their films here; this restaurant dating back to the early 1900s is a real film set. With its stucco moldings, carved marble counter, copper and opaline light fixtures, and wood paneling, you'd think it was a faithful reconstruction of old Paris. Rather provincial, the serene atmosphere is designed for eating. You can choose to be reasonable (curly *canut* cheese as a starter, bass with fennel, raspberry gratin) or to really loosen your belt and dig in (calf's head pâté), doe with horns-of-plenty wild mushrooms and *tarte tatin*. About 300 francs (45,73 €).

NEW NIOUILLAVILLE / *Imperial snack bar*
32, rue de l'Orillon, 11th arr., M° Belleville
Tel. : 01.40.21.96.18

Steaming carts rolling by, brouhaha, overheated atmosphere.... In winter you must pay a visit to this restaurant of imperial proportions where you'll love the noodle soups and steamed dumplings. Not haute cuisine, but excellent value.

LA PLANCHA / *Non-stop feria*
34, rue Keller, 11th arr., M° Bastille
Tel. : 01.48.05.20.30 ▪ Closed Sundays and Mondays ▪

When you take your place in this postage-stamp-sized restaurant, you'll feel like you're settling into the hold of a ship amidst bags of ham, red peppers, surf boards, fly-paper hanging from the ceiling, a crazy assortment of kitsch knick-knacks, and Basque folkloric items. To complete the decor, a mini-television showing bullfights, rugby matches, and pelota (the Basque national sport). Imperturbable behind the blue-ceramic tile Spanish bar, the owner cooks on his white-hot cast-iron stove tapas that arrive at the table in soup-bowl-sized dishes. You want it all to just keep coming: the mussels in lemon and olive oil, fried chippirone, potatoes in green sauce, marinated anchovies, Basque cheese with black cherry jam, and delicious green-apple liquor *(manzana)* that helps it all go down in this perpetually festive setting. About 150 francs (22,87 €).

12th arrondissement

SQUARE TROUSSEAU / *Classically hip*
1, rue Antoine-Vollon, 12th arr., M° Bastille, Ledru-Rollin
Tel. : 01.43.43.06.00

With its weathered wood, zinc bar, and bay windows opening onto the square—all of it intact from 1910 and so authentic—this bistro is the joy of the noteworthy as well as the hip (Jean-Paul Gaultier for one). At the Square Trousseau, you need not worry because the *terrine de campagne*, olive ravioli, and caramelized pork strips live up to their promises. Between 200 and 250 francs (30,49–38,11 €).

13th arrondissement

L'AVANT-GOÛT / *Daring chef*
26, rue Bobillot, 13th arr., M° Place-d'Italie
Tel.: 01.53.80.24.00 • **Closed Sundays and Mondays** •

A few steps from the place d'Italie, a young chef offers a savvy and no-nonsense cuisine. In this buttercup-colored candy shop with bright red touches that stands in sharp contrast to the external bistro decors, you'll immediately sense a tingling in your taste buds. Pork *pot-au-feu,* quail casserole with Noirmoutiers spices, *crème brûlée* with apricot compote, crisp mango-flavored cookies: a real market-based cuisine, but done so creatively! The staff is adorable and when you leave, a fifteen-minute digestive stroll will bring you straight to the galleries on rue Louise-Weiss in top spirits. About 200 francs (30,49 €).

14th arrondissement

LA FORCHETTA / *Italian good humor*
85, rue Daguerre, 14th arr., M° Gaîté
Tel.: 01.43.22.06.14

Set apart from the Gaîté-Montparnasse district, here is the sort of godsend that you're lucky to happen upon occasionally in Paris. Always packed at lunchtime despite a modest appearance (office workers mix with journalists), this little Italian place has all the freshness, amiability, and simplicity of a spot you'll return to again and again once you've discovered it. Owner Antonio Savarese is always smiling and his good spirits—after the first bites of eggplant caviar, cuttlefish-ink pasta, and other fried shrimp—are wonderfully contagious. With your taste buds awakened by a good Italian bottle of wine, you'll savor a cuisine whose soothing virtues go far beyond the simple satisfaction of your appetite.

16th arrondissement

NOURA / *Mezze on the terrace*
21, avenue Marceau, 16th arr., M° Alma-Marceau
Tel.: 01.47.20.33.33

This Lebanese place is a delicatessen, restaurant, and brasserie all in one. And it's the terrace of the last—a veritable oasis—that we recommend as a break between the Trocadéro and the Musée d'Art Moderne (museum of modern art). You'll choose from a menu of assorted plates while nibbling small olives served as an appetizer, that you might accompany with a glass of *raki* (anise-flavored alcohol) to relax you. Meatballs, *mezze* (mixed appetizers), tabouli with herbs, and hummus are all consumed with large soft pitas, and all of it for a very reasonable price (around 100 francs or 15,24 €). The idea of a Lebanese breakfast might also appeal to you: croissants with thyme, foul, and ambary juice....

19th arrondissement

LAO SIAM / *Thai delight*
49, rue de Belleville, 19th arr., M° Belleville
Tel.: 01.40.40.09.68

Local clientele and celebrities alike dine side-by-side on paper tablecloths in this Thai restaurant resembling a packed cafeteria. The beef salad with lemongrass is a sheer delight; it was out of pure gluttony that, after fish cooked in banana leaves, we ordered the caramelized dried beef that we spied on a neighboring table. An indulgence that won't weigh down either your stomach or your tab—very reasonable. About 150 francs (22,87 €).

CAFÉS

Cafés]

Places to drink, eat, read, and relax. Places to pass through or linger, neighborhood bistros, trendy cafeterias, or institutions packed with history. Cafés punctuate Parisians' daily lives for business meetings as well as dates. A place to see and be seen, to bask in the sun or sip a coffee at the counter—when is it best to leave one wonderful café to settle into another? This is what we reveal in these pages devoted largely to the loveliest terraces and clever lunch and snack spots.

1st arrondissement

ANGELINA / *Mirrors and hot chocolate*
226, rue de Rivoli, 1st arr., M° Tuileries
Tel. : 01.42.60.82.00

The place to go to sip the world's best hot chocolate or savor the legendary Mont-Blanc dessert (layers of chestnut cream, meringue, and whipped cream) as though invited for tea by a lady of the manor. The lighting, mirrors, and old-fashioned moldings alone are worth a look; when church lets out, you'd be hard-pressed to find a greater concentration of old ladies and girls in their Sunday best. Very touristy, and at the same time deliciously Parisian. To be avoided at all costs on Sundays because of the crowds.

CAFÉ LE MARLY / *At the foot of the pyramid*
93, rue de Rivoli, 1st arr., M° Palais-Royal-Musée-du-Louvre
Tel. : 01.49.26.06.60

In the living rooms of the Richelieu wing of the Louvre, Pompeiian red and slate blue contrast with the steel reflections in the furniture. Designed by Olivier Gagnère, the decoration inside isn't lacking in splendor, but you'll still fight to get one of the tables on the colonnaded terrace. Facing the Pyramid in the courtyard of the Louvre, this position offers a dreamy perspective to lose yourself in completely at the break of day. Even if the prices on the menu are pushing it (32 francs or 4,88 € for a vanilla-flavored hot milk) we'd be willing to pay dearly for this spot prized by the fashion set. Breakfast time is the best hour, when it is (relatively) less crowded and you can watch the museum line form along the fountain. You can instead take the often-neglected entrance located to the right on the other side of the intersection—and the day will begin well.

CAFÉ VERY / *Shaded break*
Jardin des Tuileries, 1st arr., M° Concorde, Tuileries
Tel. : 01.47.03.94.84

In the heart of the Tuileries gardens, a few steps from the Jeu-de-Paume gallery, you'll find an immense terrace where you can have a drink or a salad for lunch under a big parasol. On the first warm spring days, this café/restaurant is taken over by the great population of working Parisians in search of a place to sunbathe. The staff works at breakneck speed, but you can linger—reclining under the foliage of the trees—convinced that you've left Paris for a little while.

MUSCADE / *Royal gardens*
36, rue Montpensier, 1st arr., M° Palais-Royal
Tel.: 01.42.97.51.36

Benefiting from a prestigious location beneath the arcades of the Palais-Royal, this magnificent teahouse has the good grace not to make its clientele pay for the privilege of enjoying it. With the luxury of its unbeatable view of the king's gardens, Muscade has the romance of a decor that Lewis Carroll might have dreamed up. With large black-and-white checkered tiles, garnet-colored velvet panels, veined marble, and a bronzed zinc counter, the place is not lacking in spirit or taste. Copious salads and daily specials appear on the lunch menu; or, with your nose glued to the windows looking out onto the flowered groves of the park, you'll find the ultimate treat in fruit tarts and hot chocolate.

TORAYA / *Japanese refinement*
10, rue Saint-Florentin, 1st arr., M° Concorde
Tel.: 01.42.60.13.00

Utterly Japanese in the mute discretion of its beige and gray matte tones; warmed up by touches of color from the seventies-era orange armchairs and the foliage of hundred-year-old bonsai trees in the alcove. Enveloped in the polished wood of the walls and ceiling, you'll feel as though you were aboard a steamship here, on calm seas. The pleasure stems from the refinement and harmony of the place. Green teas, smoked or roasted, are accompanied by strange, lightly transparent aromatic cakes made with red beans. Each small lacquer platter is a geometric composition where the kaolin tones of the lovely Japanese dishware answer to those of the fig or apple *yokans* and the tea. Certainly don't expect to quell a sudden raging hunger here; conforming to the Japanese tradition of frugality, the portions are to be savored, but won't soothe your hunger unless you order ten at a time.

2nd arrondissement
LE CAFÉ NOIR / *Food for the soul*
65, rue Montmartre, 2nd arr., M° Les Halles
Tel.: 01.40.39.07.36

A locals' café by day, a haunt for night owls after dark, Le Café Noir—with its red interior—belongs to the category of unlikely and convivial bistros. The bar occupies half the space, and extends onto the sidewalk for aperitifs in wicker armchairs come summer. Indescribable—populated with genuine local color, the hip crowd, and grandmothers. The owner Charles, who looks like a fireman, is an amiable fellow and contributes a great deal to the appealing atmosphere of the place.

4th arrondissement

LA BELLE HORTENSE / *Literary café*
31, rue Vieille-du-Temple, 4th arr., M° Hôtel-de-Ville
Tel.: 01.48.04.71.60

Imagine.... You are wandering through the aisles of a bookstore, you hesitate over a thriller, you leaf through an anthology of Chinese short stories, and discreetly, a seat is pulled out for you and a glass of red wine handed to you while a jazz piece plays softly in the background. A golden light caresses the bottle and the book spines; the hum of animated chatter coming from the counter of La Belle Hortense stops you from discreetly taking off your shoes. Your wine resting on the corner of the table, ensconced on your bench forming a sort of narrow reading room, you can't quite bring yourself to leave the place. The wine is good, you're deeply involved with your thriller.... Only the absence of somewhat more consistent terrestrial nourishment will compel you to leave this winebar/bookstore that's as comfortable as a literary cliché.

MA BOURGOGNE / *Traditional with a view*
19, place des Vosges, 4th arr., M° Saint-Paul, Bastille
Tel.: 01.42.78.44.64

One of the oldest establishments in the place des Vosges, Ma Bourgogne's utter charm is clearly derived from its unique view of the magnificent seventeenth-century pink square. Take a seat on the heated terrace in the morning, or in the late afternoon with a pint of beer, and enjoy watching the world go by.

L'ÉBOUILLANTÉ / *Southern accent*
6, rue des Barres, 4th arr., M° Saint-Paul
Tel.: 01.42.71.09.69

You'll frequent this little café for its private and utterly unique terrace facing the Saint-Gervais church. Set upon a flight of steps linking the embankment to the town hall of the fourth arrondissement, this strategic platform in the lower part of the Marais will make you think you're in Marseille rather than Paris. After a mint tea and egg fritter *(brick aux œufs)*, you'll be ready to set off along the rocky coast again.

PASSAGE DE RETZ / *A drink before culture*
9, rue Charlot, 4th arr., M° Arts-et-Métiers
Tel.: 01.48.04.37.99

At the far end of the courtyard of a seventeenth-century private mansion, annexed to the art gallery located in what was formerly a toy-making shop, the minuscule café of the Passage de Retz is well worth your while. Entirely decorated by architect–designer Christian Blecher (who is also credited with Tsumari Chisato's boutique a few streets down), this intimate, hidden, modern-spirited café is a delightful spot with its sunny yellow furniture. You'll drink your coffee in peace, and when you leave, you can take a peek at the varied temporary exhibits of the gallery, open to the works of artists, photographers, writers, or philosophers, depending on the owner's mood.

PETIT FER À CHEVAL / *Untouched bistro*
30, rue Vieille-du-Temple, 4th arr., M° Hôtel-de-Ville
Tel.: 01.42.72.47.47

While many cafés struggle endlessly to create a retro look for themselves, the Petit Fer à Cheval didn't force it. Everything is a period piece in this neighborhood café, from the U-shaped marble and wood counter to the mosaic tile and old cast-iron radiators. Undoubtedly the most astonishing thing of all is the eternal youth of the place, a meeting spot and stopping point that has avoided the fleeting realm of trendiness and remained perpetually in vogue. Is it the casual attitude of the waiters in aprons and shirt sleeves, the mix of local and hip young clientele, the appeal evoked by the vestiges of days past? You need look no further, as you'll be perfectly content here—unless you're on the sidewalk across the street where the owner opened La Belle Hortense (see p. 42).

5th arrondissement

OUM KALTHOUM / *Hookah pipes*
4, square Vermenouze, 5th arr., M° Monge
Tel.: 01.47.87.38.58

When Oum Kalthoum's voice mingles with the aromatic smoke from the hookahs it can be raining buckets outside and the Oriental sun still manages to warm this minuscule Egyptian teahouse. During the day, the neighborhood locals inhale strawberry-flavored tobacco from the water pipes, while sipping guava or mango nectars. Come evening, the more mixed clientele chats late into the night, nibbling falafel between gulps of honey-flavored *chicha*. For a moment, you might even believe yourself to be in Cairo or Istanbul.

6th arrondissement

BAR DU MARCHÉ / *In the heart of Saint-Germain*
75, rue de Seine, 6th arr., M° Saint-Germain-des-Prés

Under frying pans hung from the ceiling, the narrow corner terrace forces you to tuck in your knees and concentrate on your conversation if you don't want to be embroiled in the one at the table right next to yours. But here you are at the very heart and center of Saint-Germain-des-Prés, at the edge of what remains of the Buci market, where it's not unusual to run into a hip young French actor or a figure from the Parisian night seeking sustenance with a *salade niçoise* or a ham omelette. The waiters are a bit much with their "Left Bank hipster" image, but are full of smiles and cheeky humor.

CAFÉ DE FLORE / *See and be seen*
172, boulevard Saint-Germain, 6th arr., M° Saint-Germain-des-Prés
Tel.: 01.45.48.55.26

What is there left to say about this mythical brasserie of Saint-Germain-des-Prés that hasn't been said before? The Japanese visit it like a museum while the Parisian intelligentsia continue to schedule their work meetings on the second floor, from which one looks out onto the intersection of Saint-Germain, framed by buckets of flowers in the windows. You can also simply have a coffee and croissant and—with newspaper in hand to make yourself less suspicious—lounge on the beige moleskin benches on the lookout for famous faces.

CAFÉ DE LA MAIRIE / *Front-row seats*
85, place Saint-Sulpice, 6th arr., M° Saint-Sulpice
Tel.: 01.43.26.67.82

You should find a seat on the terrace of the Café de la Mairie in the early hours of the day. The cane chairs are lined up in rows facing Saint-Sulpice church, giving the impression that you are part of an audience waiting for the curtain to rise. At daybreak, this is a lovely place to sit and watch the show of Paris waking up. The golden light that bathes the square, the animated coming-and-going of the shopkeepers, publishers, and then the chic and stylish ladies of the neighborhood getting ready for a day of shopping.... This is a place to go to ease gently into the day.

Chapter 3

LA PALETTE / *Beaux-Arts students*
43, rue de Seine, 6th arr., M° Saint-Germain-des-Prés
Tel. : 01.43.26.68.15

The lack of humor in the waiters, the service often reduced to a bare minimum, archaic bathrooms—you swear to yourself every time that it's the last time, and yet....You always find yourself back at La Palette. Situated in the heart of Saint-Germain, this mystery of Parisian life stems from the brasserie's powerful charm that retains—besides the polish of its woodwork weathered with time—the vivid memory of the artistic effervescence of the early twentieth century.The room and terrace, heated and always packed, remain the unshakable meeting spots for the well-to-do gallery owners of the neighborhood and the rowdy students of the Beaux-Art (Paris's foremost art school). Saturated with noise and history, the atmosphere will make you forget the lapses of a staff that upholds the cliché of Paris as a rude city.

LA RHUMERIE / *Hot milk punch*
166, boulevard Saint-Germain, 6th arr., M° Saint-Germain-des-Prés
Tel. : 01.43.54.28.94

Simone de Beauvoir came here to warm up her winter evenings with a hot milk punch.After a movie at one of the cinemas near the Odéon, we do the same.A bit raised like an embarkation plank, with its wooden terrace open on mild summer evenings, La Rhumerie could be a tourist trap, but blessedly it's not. For 100 francs (15,24 €), you'll love the Creole platter (acras, blood sausage, minced and spiced fish) and a glass of punch.

LE ROSTAND / *By the fireside*
6, place Edmond-Rostand, 6th arr., M° Odéon
Tel. : 01.43.54.61.58

A café where a real fire burns in the hearth—after a jog or a chilly stroll in the Luxembourg gardens, what a pleasure to come here to warm up in front of the crackling fireplace of this charming room remodeled in the colors of Provence. In jeans and white aprons, the waiters set the casual tone of the place.As relaxing as a Sunday afternoon.

7th arrondissement

LE BASILE / *Students' hangout*
34, rue de Grenelle, 7th arr., M° Rue-du-Bac
Tel. : 01.42.22.59.46

"But it's a students' cafeteria!" we exclaimed upon entering this funny refectory lit in red, yellow, and pink neon. The waiter who took our order smiled: shepherd's pie and green bean salad with salmon, all perfectly satisfying. Radio Latina in the background, the brouhaha of a schoolyard at recess, and fifties-era details—truly unusual and totally successful, resembling a sitcom version of a student cafeteria in the heart of the seventh arrondissement.

8th arrondissement

HANDMADE / *Good concept*
19, rue Jean-Mermoz, 8th arr., M° Franklin-Roosevelt
Tel. : 01.45.62.50.05 ▪ Open from 8 A.M. to 5 P.M. ▪

For anyone who has ever known the anxiety of erring onto the Champs-Élysées at lunchtime on an empty stomach between two meetings, the opening of this little-known snack bar will be excellent news. The recipe for the leek soup is from French author Marguerite Duras, the grain breads from Kaizer, the preserves the same as those served at the Ritz in London, the cheeses those that Alain Ducasse himself serves. The quiches, sandwiches, grated carrots, fruits, cakes, and other dishes—to be consumed at a small oak table or to go—are indeed handmade. From the stainless steel flatware to the handblown glasses and handmade porcelain coffee cups, all of it is created by craftsmen and sold on location. Open from 8 A.M. to 5 P.M., this mini-version of Ducasse's Spoon (see p. 32) is full of spirit and creativity. You'll easily breakfast or lunch for under 80 francs (12,20 €) in a remarkably elaborate setting.

11th arrondissement

CAFÉ DU PASSAGE / *Designer jazz*
12, rue de Charonne, 11th arr., M° Bastille
Tel. : 01.49.29.97.64

Gérard, the café's host with newly discovered decorator talents, explains jokingly that he wanted to create a "bar that would be comfortable for the old people" in the Bastille, the favorite arrondissement of Parisian youth.

Highly valued by the forty-year-olds in the neighborhood (it's the headquarters of the architects of Faubourg-Saint-Antoine and you might come upon Lacroix or Gaultier, who are both locals), this bar—open from 6 P.M. to 2 A.M.—is actually atypical on a street where you'll find primarily trendy bars serving strong, fancy drinks. In a jazzy, muted atmosphere that successfully mixes the British chic of smooth armchairs with touches of Italian design, you'll sip from the vintages described on the endless and intentionally literary menu. If you get hungry as the evening extends late into the night, you can snack on some clever appetizer or from a top-quality cheese plate.

LE CHARBON / *Trendy retro*
109, rue Oberkampf, 11th arr., M° Oberkampf
Tel.: 01.43.57.55.13

Formerly a music hall transformed into a movie house, Le Charbon was promoted as a "trendy bar" when it reopened in 1995. In addition to that rather ephemeral quality, the café is appealing for its high ceilings, kept intact with the exception of the magnificent copper light fixtures hung upside down and the piece of furniture from a hosiery shop set up behind the counter. The ghost ship of a lost "people's Paris," Le Charbon offers deliberately casual and familiar service, out of ironic respect for the (rare) clientele in coat-and-tie searching for a change of scenery. The waiters, informal and affectionate in their overalls, set the tone—and don't hesitate to acknowledge that the mediocre quality of the food remains a weak point. But the kitchen is undergoing a restructuring; stay posted....

12th arrondissement

LE VIADUC CAFÉ / *Space as a luxury*
43, avenue Daumesnil, 12th arr., M° Gare-de-Lyon, Ledru-Rollin
Tel.: 01.44.74.70.70

In winter for its cathedral arches and copious Sunday jazz brunches. In summer for its southern-spirited terrace—an ideal people-watching spot under rectangular parasols. This is a welcome stop that can be combined with a stroll up the hill. There's little point, however, in window-shopping at the galleries set up under the neighboring arcades: the site is sumptuous, but the contents of the boutiques leave something to be desired.

Nightlife

"I don't go out..." is often the sad and heartfelt reply to the eternal question, "Where do you go out in Paris?" Whether this is the coy response of a night owl or a genuine admission, the important thing is to recognize that since the end of the eighties and the closing of the legendary Palace nightclub, Parisian nights are primarily spent in bars and restaurants, often ending in private parties. This chapter therefore proposes a great many cocktail lounges and sketches the geopolitics of the electronic music scene in all its glory. From bars to clubs to barges along the banks of the Seine, from Barbès to Bastille—the DJs, guests, and inhabitants define an eclectic and exciting nightlife well worth discovering.

BARS
1st arrondissement
LE FUMOIR / *Cocktails and muted tones*
6, rue de l'Amiral-Coligny, 1st arr., M° Louvre-Rivoli
Tel.: 01.42.92.00.24

With its Chesterfield armchairs and couches, wide thirties-era fans, and sepia-toned harmony, Le Fumoir is without question one of the most beautiful bars in Paris in terms of style and size. Aside from the quasi-infinite choice of cocktails, whiskies, and other drinks, you'll note the wonderful attention to detail: claw-footed champagne buckets, blinds filtering the sunlight, exotic flowers, jazz playing in the background. At the back, a library lit with Chinese lanterns invites you to linger—a thriller or art book in hand—in a cozy and luxurious setting reminiscent of the colonial bars of years gone by. In the evening, the fairytale view of the Louvre all lit up reminds you that you are indeed in Paris, not New York.

LE ROYAL MONDÉTOUR / *So fashionable*
14, rue Mondétour, 1st arr., M° Étienne-Marcel
Tel.: 01.42.36.85.50

A cross between a disco and an intergalactic station, with its poof-cushion seats and celestial blue lights, this bar/restaurant has become the darling of the members of the fashion world—who head there in droves during the shows. The lineup of stylish accessories and Prada outfits is a fascinating sight to behold for anyone whose curiosity is piqued by this kind of scene, but this place is less about seeing than being seen. From 11 P.M. on, the clientele consists of an eclectic mix of night owls, DJs of the moment, and veterans of the eighties. The volume of the house music rises and the tables are pushed aside to improvise a dance floor. This is a place to frequent during the week or on Sundays for theme nights (tandoori chicken and Indian vibes, Tokyo night with sushi, paella for Latin nights).

2nd arrondissement
HARRY'S NEW YORK BAR / *Whisky bar*
5, rue Daunou, 2nd arr., M° Opéra
Tel.: 01.42.61.71.14

An eternal classic of the Parisian night scene (the Existentialists used to come here to knock back their scotch), where the Bloody Mary was created. With its glossy varnished woodwork, flags and coats of arms from

American colleges, and deep red moleskin benches, this is an utterly relaxing hot spot if you're in the mood to indulge in one bourbon after another while stuffing yourself with peanuts.

3rd arrondissement

LE DÉTOUR / *Mediterranean hideaway*
5, rue Elvézir, 3rd arr., M° Saint-Paul
Tel.: 01.40.29.44.04

In a truly deserted area of the Marais, this new spot is trying to warm up its deep, beautiful space with Mediterranean colors, a terracotta floor, and off-white walls with a touch of faded blue. With its wrought iron light fixtures and red and orange velvet seats, you could be in Barcelona or Tangiers. In the basement, a small musical club/bar hopes to become the meeting lounge of choice on Sunday nights for the tired heroes of Parisian nightlife, hip radio journalists, and in-vogue DJs. If the idea takes—and it really is rather appealing—it will certainly be worth the detour.

WEB BAR / *Theme nights*
32, rue de Picardie, 3rd arr., M° Temple
Tel.: 01.42.72.66.55

Psychology, multimedia, literature, art: the Web Bar is raising the level of nightlife a notch with its ambitious theme nights rather like televised academic debates. In the basement of what was formerly a garment factory, half-concrete, half-metal, an entire team works on renewing and sustaining the success of a somewhat helter-skelter event-based program. During the day, web addicts settle in with their backs to the room facing the computers on the upper level, which gives you the strange impression that you have stumbled upon the cafeteria of a start up. In the evenings, girls and boys from the Temple neighborhood come to have a drink and fill up on *carpaccio*, learn Salsa on Mondays in a jam-packed dance room, or reinvent the world to the background music of "mix on the web."

6th arrondissement

L'AZ BAR, BAR DE L'ALCAZAR / *Lounge atmosphere*
62, rue Mazarine, 6th arr., M° Odéon
Tel.: 01.53.10.19.99

A nice save for Terence Conran's London-style brasserie, whose widely publicized opening was tremendously disappointing. Not only has the food improved, but thanks to the musical program on the mezzanine overlooking the restaurant, the place is in the midst of reinventing itself. Through a fantastic entry hall and up a staircase bordered with open dishes of fresh flowers, you reach the second floor without losing sight of the diners on the first floor—like a false bottom in the form of an atrium that overlooks the bar, lit during the day by a vast skylight. With small designer velvet armchairs, a cozy atmosphere, soft lighting, and a lavish cocktail menu, we like the stylish serenity of this place that is rapidly becoming a must of the electronic lounge scene.

10th arrondissement
L'OPUS / *More jazz than glitter*
167, quai de Valmy, 10th arr., M° Louis-Blanc
Tel.: 01.40.34.70.00

A former mess hall for British officers, the Opus Café made its mark in the eighties, then fell into complete obscurity. Over a year ago the team changed and now plays a score featuring jazz, soul, and funk without any glittery effects. The place—vast under its high ceilings, with an old wooden dancing floor, red curtains, ship's rail ropes, and restaurant on the mezzanine—is really superb, and makes you want to pass by it at a distance simply to soak in its peaceful setting and excellent music. Something worth following up on since the idea is still in the works: leisurely Sunday brunches where there will supposedly be a rag-bag medley of concerts, shows, and short films presented throughout the day.

11th arrondissement
LE CHINA CLUB / *Thirties Shanghai*
50, rue de Charenton, 11th arr., M° Ledru-Rollin, Bastille
Tel.: 01.43.43.82.02

This fantastic bar's sophisticated decor is reminiscent of Shanghai in the thirties. You cross the restaurant—dark velvet drapes and a black-and-white checkered floor—to reach the lacquered doors leading to the bar on the next floor. Dim lighting and candle haloes, Chesterfield couches, wood-slatted blinds, Chinese furnishings—as a cigarette vendor passes by with her wares in a basket slung around her neck, you'd think you were in the sitting room of an imperial hotel. Right in the Bastille, this is a real haven of elegance and comfort and ideal for savoring excellent cocktails with Haydn, Tchaikovski, and Dvorák playing in the background—in a setting that is utterly relaxing despite (or thanks to?) the elegance of the premises.

LA FABRIQUE / *Good sets, fine beer*
53, rue du Faubourg-Saint-Antoine, 11th arr., M° Ledru-Rollin, Bastille
Tel.: 01.43.07.67.07

Like many Parisian nightspots, La Fabrique could benefit from a fresh coat of paint, but the effort put into welcoming you and the high quality of the music will make you forget the tired look of the place. The first room, along a bar where you can savor house-brewed organic beer, leads to a second one, which is quite vast and devoted to the restaurant (nice effort on the menu), where journalists and the "hip and stylish" of the neighborhood flock at lunchtime. In the evenings, the place is given over to music, for electronic mixes and futuristic jazz by promising young DJs (Demon, Lady Bird) and more well-known names (Charles Schilling, Pompougnac). On Sundays, a lavish brunch is served with live jazz in the background.

HOTEL BARS
1st arrondissement

BAR HEMINGWAY, HÔTEL RITZ / *Hemingway's bar*
38, rue Cambon, 1st arr., M° Madeleine
Tel.: 01.43.16.30.30

You must cross the entire Ritz and its airport-like corridor of shops to find the marvelous bar so dear to Ernest Hemingway. F. Scott Fitzgerald made this bar known to Hemingway in the twenties; he became instantly smitten with it and made it his *pied-à-terre* in Paris. History has it that on August 25, 1944, Hemingway arrived in the hotel of the place Vendôme flanked by an armed escort and absolutely determined to deliver it from its German occupants. The latter having already left the premises, the commando operation ended up at the bar (situated at the back of the hotel by the rue Cambon entrance) where it celebrated the Liberation of Paris with champagne. A real break in habit for the author—whose regular drink was a dry Martini, often consumed one after another. Today, Collin P. Field—worthy inheritor of the dynasty of barmen at the Ritz—prepares this classic drink in glasses frozen at -18.4° centigrade (-1° Fahrenheit), so that the ice cubes do not melt and alter the quality of the beverage. The same fanatical care presides over the creation of house classics and recent concoctions developed by Collin, such as the *benderitter*, a "perfect cocktail" with a base of champagne. Ensconced between two silk cushions and with Josephine Baker on the turntable, you will believe without a doubt that Hemingway, "when he dreamed of Paradise, always found himself transported to the Ritz."

LE CAFÉ DE VENDÔME / *Plush piano bar*
1, place Vendôme, 1st arr., M° Concorde, Tuileries, Opéra
Tel. : 01.55.04.55.55

On the second floor of a brand new hotel—verging on being a bit too flashy with its gleaming marble floors and shiny gilding—the Café Vendôme has the air of a private British club. Once seated at one of the alcove tables looking out on the place Vendôme, you will forget the overly glittery aspect of this luxurious place and savor its muted atmosphere. Chesterfield couches, Scottish-motif carpeting, dark wood paneling, a fireplace—you'll quickly be won over by the cozy sitting room, where a pianist arrives at cocktail hour.

8th arrondissement

MATHI'S / *Jet-set only*
3, rue de Ponthieu, 8th arr., M° Champs-Élysées-Clemenceau
Tel. : 01.53.76.01.62

A red rococo decor and a decadent Parisian atmosphere reigns in this hotel bar, which opens its doors at 10 P.M. to a more or less wild client-ele of regulars, party-goers, hipsters, and stars of the eighties—who are all right at home here. A meeting place where you can simply go as an ethnologist curious about society life, or to join in the fun if you've got a real affinity for the "dahling" spirit of the place.

CLUBS
2nd arrondissement

LE REX CLUB / *Techno hype*
5, boulevard Poissonnière, 2nd arr., M° Grands-Boulevards
Tel. : 01.42.36.10.96

Under the starry arch of the Rex, the rock program gave way to the best of the experimental electronic scene. From Bains to Batofar, all of techno Paris meets up here on Thursday nights to commune to the pulsing of decibels.

3rd arrondissement

LES BAINS / *Twenty years of Parisian nightlife*
7, rue du Bourg-l'Abbé, 3rd arr., M° Étienne-Marcel
Tel. : 01.48.87.01.80

With its VIPs and house music, the Paris club most well-known to foreigners is turning twenty years old—a respectable age that confers upon it the ambiguous status of being a Parisian institution. At the helm, David and Kathy Guetta do a lot to avoid the pitfalls of "trendy" music which gets crowds moving about as much as figures in the Musée Grévin (Paris's wax museum)—he, by assuring a rotation of high-end DJs and she, by being a well-known figure of the nightclub world from Ibiza to Paris. At the very stylish Thai restaurant overlooking the room for "black music" Wednesdays, you might run into Catherine Deneuve or Lauren Bacall, Lenny Kravitz or Puff Daddy—as well as droves of celebrities at the super-exclusive club on the second floor.

LE TANGO / *Anything could happen*
11, rue au Maire, 3rd arr., M° Arts-et-Métiers
Tel. : 01.42.72.17.78

A country dance-hall atmosphere pervades this minuscule club with its wholesome, exhilarating spirit. Moleskin benches surround the floor where a series of tangos, *passo doble*, and waltzes alternate with old eighties mixes. Occasionally, an impromptu drag performance on the balcony adds to the somewhat crazy sixties' spirit of the place. You'll have a fun time here, with a rare mix of late-night revelers who seem to have passed the word on to each other.

8th arrondissement

QUEEN / *French touch*
102, avenue des Champs-Élysées, 8th arr., M° George-V
Tel. : 01.53.89.08.90

It all began in October 1996 with the first "Respect" evening: at the turntables was Daft Punk; six months later his album would be released and sell over a million copies. The hip media from across the Channel identified the famous "French touch" and Queen transformed itself into the headquarters of the Parisian techno scene. The "Respect" turntables continue to spin between New York and Copenhagen, but have been replaced at Queen by "secret" nights on Wednesdays. Dimitri from Paris, Ivan, and Romain cultivate a house disco without concession here, open some evenings for stimulating improvisations to a few passing guests.

STRIP TEASE / *Twenty-first-century cabaret*
49, rue de Ponthieu, 8th arr., M° Franklin-Roosevelt

David Guetta's latest idea! Recreate the cabaret of the new millennium in Paris, a cross between the Lido and Demi Moore's *Strip Tease*. With a designer look warmed up by crimson theatrical curtains, girls from all corners of the earth fan out according to an erotic ritual "to be taken tongue-in-cheek," says the man in charge. With a ferocious selection process at the entrance and sublime creatures sauntering between the tables of the dumbfounded guests, this new spot could become terribly trendy, or touristy. Watch this space....

13th arrondissement

LE BATOFAR / *Legendary after-hours*
Facing 11, quai François-Mauriac, 13th arr., M° Bibliothèque-François-Mitterrand
Tel.: 01.56.29.10.00

This barge repainted in bright red is a surrealistic sight moored on the banks of the Seine. In the summer it's a real joy to have a drink on the deck, far from the city's congested arteries; very far, it seems, from Paris altogether. But the fame of the Batofar goes well beyond the charm of its location. Known also for its "Kwality" events (two Sundays a month, six nonstop hours of deep house music without any risk of complaints from neighbors), it draws a crowd of technophiles, beautiful people, intellectuals, and other hip folks attracted like late-night butterflies to the perceptible cult aroma of the out-of-this-world music sessions.

17th arrondissement

TGV – THANK GOD I'M A VIP / *Mingle with VIPs*
39, avenue de Wagram, 17th arr., M° Ternes

"Multi-ethnic and Parisian" because, explains the coordinator, you're just as likely to run into high society as the hip-hop suburban youth during the Sylvie Chataignier evenings—absolutely one of the showiest in Paris. A sacred event for the fashion and club worlds, these evenings are nevertheless open to the uninformed who want to feel like they "belong." Past the metal barriers on the sidewalk, red carpets and potted palms set the exclusive Monaco-style tone of this bimonthly event. Inside, the heady aromas of incense, the disco ball suspended from the center of the crystal light fixtures, theatrical colonnades, and crimson crushed velvet all contribute to the stylish atmosphere of the Wagram room—rather opulent compared to the typical shabbiness of Parisian nights. The nobodies keep an eye out for the beautiful people, who take Polaroid pictures of themselves as souvenirs.

18th arrondissement

LE DIVAN DU MONDE / *Mixes*
75, rue des Matyrs, 18th arr., M° Pigalle
Tel.: 01.44.92.77.66

With its airs of a shabby Italian theater, Le Divan du Monde is the most eclectic concert hall in Paris. From the traditional Jamaican sound system to North African music—as well as the Brazilian fiestas, world music, French rock, and jungle music—no evening and no audience are alike. Far from the showy and glamorous spots, this big cabaret appeals for its somewhat sloppy look and ever-changing musical program. You go for the pleasure of mingling and discovering a Moroccan diva or an African percussionist, without a worry about showing up in jeans and sneakers.

L'ÉLYSÉE-MONTMARTRE /
Dream venue with great acoustics
72, boulevard de Rochechouart, 18th arr., M° Anvers
Tel.: 01.44.92.45.45

A historically preserved facade and a structure designed by Eiffel, L'Élysée-Montmartre does not settle for just being one of the most beautiful halls in Paris—in the style typical of a historical monument with stucco moldings patinaed by smoke—but also boasts that it has one of the best sounds in the city, with good reason. The sandbags that shore up the stage and the positioning of the speakers create powerful and enveloping acoustics. Twice a month, the ball led by the Grand Orchestre and DJ Nouredine offers an evening similar to "Saturday night variety shows" with a background of French songs and international hits—a live variation on a family night in front of the TV or a night with the neighbors. But the absolute *must* of the moment remains the Kings nights (the star DJs of the moment, from Laurent Garnier to Daft Punk) and La Scream, based on the seven original sins. The hip gay crowd assembles here in droves for the wild live performances (a crucified Christ figure on a big illuminated cross ravaged by a lecherous devil as a pagan parable of lust) and cutting-edge house mixes. The scene is also to be found in the guests themselves, who all contribute to the Village People atmosphere.

ARTS

Arts]

It's hard to count the number of galleries that have set up shop between the rue de Seine and the rue de Beaune—they seem to form an open-air museum whose evening and Sunday openings attract an increasing number of passers-by in a sort of giant and informal cultural event. From the avenue Matignon to the back courtyards of the Marais, contemporary art is now developing in the east part of the city around the rue Louise-Weiss (see p. 68), with avant-garde exhibits in the middle of nowhere—a geographical shift akin to an institutionalized happening. Video installations, cyber-art sculptures, Chinese dissident painters, Oceanic art, conceptual photography, exhibited treasures in little-known museums, leading galleries, private foundations, and trendy record dealers: Paris is bursting with images, shapes, and sounds.

ALEXANDRE BIAGGI / *Esthetic nostalgia*
14, rue de Seine, 6th arr., M° Saint-Germain-des-Prés
Tel.: 01.44.07.34.73

Specializing in twentieth-century furniture, this gallery is visited like a shrine. Powdery white with heavy pink velvet curtains, it carries a high-end selection of the trendiest forties-era designers (J.-M. Frank, Riccardi), occasionally punctuated by eclectic finds: eighteenth-century light fixtures in colored crystal and the graceful molds of sculptures from the Broussard castle. Alexandre Biaggi strolls about, natty and nonchalant and nostalgic for the thirties....

ANTOINE DE VILMORIN / *A guide in the art jungle*
Tel.: 01.42.61.94.24 / 06.11.88.12.07

A specialist in seventeenth-century Italian paintings, Antoine de Vilmorin is an auctioneer-turned-consultant. Although not an art dealer himself, he advises wealthy individuals, art lovers, and collectors seeking to make an informed purchase. To discern his clients' tastes, he often takes them out to survey Paris's museums before venturing into the galleries and auction halls that are so familiar to him. "My strength is in my discretion," smiles this confident thirty-year-old. Avoid the traps of a doubtful provenance, check the pedigree of an old master painting, judge the fairness of the price.... The art market is a fascinating treasure hunt for this member of the European Chamber of Experts. Paid by commission, this one-off consultant is appealing for his calm erudition and his elegant skills in educating neophytes.

LES ARCADES / *Twentieth-century masters*
8, rue de Castiglione, 1st arr., M° Concorde
Tel.: 01.42.60.62.96

Five years ago, Yves Lebouc's children took over this excellent bookstore dedicated to the great twentieth-century masters—Chagall, Matisse, Braque, Dubuffet, Giacometti, Picasso, Léger—and hardcover bound volumes. With its green bronze wood paneling and shelves stretching high above you, this half-antiquated, half-designer shop is overflowing with treasures. You'll leaf delicately through a *Matière et Mémoire* signed by Jean Dubuffet or a Max Jacob text illustrated with the powerful watercolors of Picasso—rare pieces and real works of art for which you'll ask the price merely out of curiosity. More reasonable are the limited-edition copies from the "Paquebot" collection, containing some lovely lithographs.

C.T. LOO & COMPANY / *Far East*
48, rue de Courcelles, 8th arr., M° Saint-Philippe-du-Roule
Tel.: 01.45.62.53.15

Five minutes from the Jacquemart-André museum (see p. 67), surrounded by Haussmann-era buildings, stands a brick-colored pagoda. Beyond the iron portal, you ring to gain access to the gallery on the first floor. In a long, two-level hall, sublime pieces of Chinese, Japanese, and Korean art from the era of Tang and Meiji are soberly presented, along with more recent pieces. The ceramic platters and lacquer ware by Rosanjin exhibited recently, for example, are a fine illustration of the Japanese esthetic of "perfect modesty."

DOMINIQUE DE ROQUEMAUREL-GALITZINE /
Back from Russia
12, rue de Clichy, 9th arr., M° Trinité
Tel: 01.40.23.03.80

Four birchwood display windows resembling reliquaries frame the edges of the living room (lit by a sumptuous Murano light fixture), from which you'll hear the sounds of hushed consultations. Dominique de Roquemaurel receives visitors in her fabulous Haussmann-style apartment by appointment only and is known the world over by collectors of Russian-made eggs. In gold, diamond, and porcelain, you'll discover jeweled eggs mounted as pendants, hung from ribbons, and delicately resting on velvet cushions—from miniature to ostrich egg in size. Nicknamed "the countess of hats," she also designs her own jewelry made in Russia. Assembled from old-fashioned cameos, coral, rubies, and emeralds and set in gold or silver, these are original creations with the false airs of old family heirlooms.

DROUOT / *Auctioneer*
9, rue Drouot, 9th arr., M° Richelieu-Drouot
Tel.: 01.48.00.20.20

This famous auction house should be visited in two steps. In the morning, thread your way among the secondhand goods dealers with their hair tied back with string and antique dealers in their double-breasted jackets, all armed with a notebook and pencil, in a great jumble of carpets, light fixtures, furniture, and display windows crammed with objects like curiosity cabinets. The next day, or the day after that, it will all be for sale. At noon, everyone scatters to one of the cafés in the area to plan their strategy and negotiate in hushed tones. At 2 P.M., the doors reopen to the crowd, which pushes inside in hopes of gaining access to one of the few available seats.

It's best to be seated if you plan to participate in the sale of the day, which is punctuated by knocks of the gavel and the commentary—often quite funny—of the auctioneers. A sudden acceleration of bids, dead time, murmurs of approval from the audience.... It's a real spectacle, where you can still hope to unearth that rare pearl at the bottom of a bin of linens or loose dishware.

FONDATION CARTIER / *Contemporary patronage*
261, boulevard Raspail, 14th arr., M° Raspail
Tel.: 01.42.18.56.50 ▪ Open from noon to 8 P.M.; closed Mondays ▪

This building designed by Jean Nouvel is a mix of glass facades and metal framework. On the lookout for anything new in the world of fashion, design, photography, and contemporary art in general, the Fondation Cartier is as easy to visit as a department store. Is it the transparency and luminous quality of the place, the somewhat wild beauty of the garden that surrounds it, or its proximity to the street? We don't really know, but you enter freely, without the least hesitation. To encourage this spirit of discovery, exciting "Nomadic" evenings are organized every Thursday, focusing on visiting designers, artists, and musicians.

FONDATION DAPPER / *Splendors of Africa*
50, avenue Victor-Hugo, 16th arr., M° Victor-Hugo
Tel.: 01.45.00.07.48 ▪ Open from 11 A.M. to 7 P.M. ▪

After entering through the door of a fashionable building, you'll discover this museum hidden within a minuscule mansion at the far end of a rectangular courtyard planted with bamboo. On three narrow, renovated floors with polished parquet and dim lighting, you'll find the most beautiful exhibit of statues and African objects in Paris. Always thematically based, with the most exceptional pieces displayed to do them justice, the visit most often ends with the purchase of one of the catalogs sold at the entrance. Beautiful art books.

FRANCK / *Images of an era*
14, rue des Pyramides, 1st arr., M° Pyramides
Tel.: 01.42.60.65.13

Specializing in contemporary art—Carl André, Natacha Lesueur, Nobuyoshi Araki, Arianne Lopez, Pierrette Bloch—this gallery intends to keep a critical and vigilant eye on its era. Once a year, free reign is given to one important collector to set up a show, like Gilles Fuchs—who develops his sense of humor through the works of Raymond Hains, Fabrice Hybert, Anne Ferrer, Eric Duyckaerts, and Natacha Lesueur.

FRÉDÉRIC SANCHEZ / *Fashion hangout*
5, rue Sainte-Anastase, 4th arr., M° Hôtel-de-Ville
Tel.: 01.44.54.92.04

Fred Bladou and Frederic Sanchez have worked for Martin Margiela, Martine Sitbon, Jean-Paul Gaultier, Jil Sander, Louis Vuitton, Yves Saint Laurent, and a number of others. These two are "sound providers" of the fashion shows, the new generation of stars inseparable from the vanity of ready-to-wear as seen by Altman. In search of Parisian offices, and always sought out by the small fashion crowd— "Fred, where did you unearth this great oldie?"—they decided to create a space that would be open to the public: you can listen to their favorite CDs (from *Peter and the Wolf* by Prokoviev to the latest sounds by Stereolab) displayed on the wall like prints. You can observe discussions between designers and musicians and stroll through the photo exhibits. The gallery, a long immaculate white corridor set up under a skylight in the Marais, is also worthwhile for the gossip of the stylists and the latest news on the designers: it's here that the newsletter of fashion is written. "If we were in New York, we would be between Chelsea and the West Village," sums up Frederic Sanchez.

GALERIE D'ARCHITECTURE / *Chic urbanism*
11, rue des Blancs-Manteaux, 4th arr., M° Hôtel-de-Ville
Tel.: 01.49.96.64.00

The two architects who founded this place, Gian Mauro and Olga, take exceptional care of it. The day we were there, they were repainting the walls of their superb loft as they awaited the opening of their next exhibit. Molded plastic chairs, display shelves, tables—from floor to ceiling, everything is so immaculately white that it becomes almost invisible. As a result, the designs, photographs, and blueprints of the young architects presented here stand out all the more. Evening events, conferences, and debates will animate this gallery that dreams of building something of tomorrow's world—a very conceptual place with its café, library, and bookstore.

GALERIE BELLE ET BELLE / *Affordable prints*
31, rue de Seine, 6th arr., M° Saint-Germain-des-Prés
Tel.: 01.43.25.77.24

A small gallery, Belle et Belle (referring to the *belles-sœurs,* the sisters-in-law who are partners in this enterprise) carries a lovely selection of twentieth-century painters: Sonia Delauney, Alechinsky, Chagall, Oliver Debré.... Don't hesitate to dive into the lithographs by Fernand Léger and Matta—they are reasonably priced.

LA GALERIE DU CACHEMIRIEN / *Travel on the spot*
38, rue de Seine, 6th arr., M° Saint-Germain-des-Prés
Tel.: 01.40.51.83.30

This stationary caravan, a recent annex of the Boutique du Cachemerien, sumptuously sets the scene for mixing fabrics (unique nineteenth-century pieces, pashmina from Kashmir, brocades, the knotted silk of Persian carpets) with objects (Milanese ceramics, leather boxes from Tibet), furnishings (Art Deco sofas made of walnut wood), and finally, the work of a specially selected artist exhibited for his or her vision and modern sense of style. The two adjoining, handsome rooms give an impression of great depth—with their harmony and poetic rarity, there's no overcrowding. It's virtually impossible not to emerge with something from this shop, be it a stunning shawl or a lightweight silk robe from the Dream Wear collection.

GALERIE DE FRANCE / *Safe investments and dissidents*
54, rue de la Verrerie, 4th arr., M° Hôtel-de-Ville
Tel.: 01.42.74.38.00

At its opening in 1942, the Galerie de France positioned itself to be favorable to young, independent painters. During the fifties, the names Alechinsky, Hartung, Poliakoff, Soulages, Zao Wou-ki, Pollock, De Kooning, and Kline all peppered an exceptional list of exhibitors. Set up for the last twenty years on the rue de la Verrerie, today it exhibits artists such as Gilles Aillaud, Martial Raysse, J.-P. Pincemin, and Nikki de Saint-Phalle and maintains, through the impetus of the attractive Xin-Dong Chen, tight links with the new generation of young Chinese dissident artists whose powerful and surprising installations regularly occupy the place.

GALERIE 213 MARION DE BEAUPRÉ /
Contemporary photography
213, boulevard Raspail, 14th arr., M° Vavin
Tel.: 01.43.22.83.23

A longtime agent for fashion photographers, Marion de Beaupré opened her own gallery two years ago—the only one in Paris to exclusively present living artists. On the second floor of an apartment with naked walls and a cement floor hang the works of young photographers—Elain Constantine, Mario Sorrenti, Camille Vivier, Elger Esser—alternating with those of confirmed artists such as Patrick Michel, Dawid, Jean-François Lepage, and Paolo Roversi. Her excellent choices (the value of Elger Esser's works almost doubled in a couple of months), her bias for artistic relevance and fashion, and her openness to on-the-rise talents make this a much-talked-of place on the frontiers of contemporary art. On the first floor, the specialized bookstore—a former brasserie dating back to the beginning of the twentieth century—should be visited for its superb and intact Art Deco woodwork.

GALERIE MEYER / *Tribal art*
17, rue des Beaux-Arts, 6th arr., M° Saint-Germain-des-Prés
Tel.: 01.43.54.85.74

Perhaps you've already stopped dead in front of the two sumptuous volumes of *Oceanic Art* published by Könemann (1999). The author of this work, Anthony J. P. Meyer, is also the founder of this Saint-Germain-des-Prés gallery, where some very handsome masks, lances, and statuettes of the Maori (New Zealand), Asmat and Sepik (Papua New Guinea), and natives of the islands of Vanuatu and New Ireland are on display. The prices are eloquent proof of the inevitable scarcity of primitive art. You should also visit the Musée des Art d'Afrique et d'Océanie (293, avenue Daumesnil, 12th arr.).

INSTITUT DU MONDE ARABE / *Architectural wonder*
1, rue des Fossés-Saint-Bernard, 5th arr., M° Jussieu, Cardinal-Lemoine
Tel.: 01.40.51.38.38 • Open from 10 A.M. to 6 P.M.; closed Mondays •

Designed by architect Jean Nouvel, the Institut du Monde Arabe is the building that finally reconciled Parisians with modern architecture. An anchored cruise ship by the Seine whose flanks seem to hug the curve of the river, it still feels entirely contemporary even twelve years after its inauguration. With its southern facade made up of ingenious metal diaphragms that open and close according to the amount of natural light (a high-tech transcription of traditional Eastern *mushrabeyeh,* or wooden window lattices), spiral white marble tower for the books, and clear glass elevators—the entire building is a web of walkways between East and West. You absolutely must go up to the roof terrace, where it's cliché—but true—to say that it offers one of the loveliest views of Paris and Notre-Dame.

JÉRÔME DE NOIRMONT / *Contemporary poetry*
38, avenue Matignon, 8th arr., M° Franklin-Roosevelt
Tel.: 01.42.89.89.00

The avenue Matignon is to art what the avenue Montaigne is to fashion: the opulent galleries are lined up along the sidewalk and thronged by an elegant and busy crowd. Opened in 1994, the Jérôme de Noirmont gallery initially decided to make a name for itself by presenting the known values of the eighties (including an Andy Warhol retrospective), and currently is focused on the discovery of new talent. After a homage to New York artist Keith Haring, the Brigitte Nahon and Shirin Neshat exhibits attracted a lot of attention. Exclusively and permanently, the works of David Mach and Pierre et Gilles set the tone—more dreamy than violent—of this outpost of contemporary art.

MAÏ OLIVIER / Carismatic gallery owner
51, rue Sainte-Croix-de-la-Bretonnerie, 4th arr., M° Hôtel-de-Ville
Tel.: 01.48.04.09.60

A superb woman whose enthusiasm is contagious, Maï Olivier is getting ahead largely because of her emotion and great instincts. The result is a generous eclecticism: the luminous cyber art cases by Diane Harris are followed by paintings of crushed bark by Siaket Mafoi, then grating sculptures on watercolor paper by Oreste Zevola and graceful forged iron ones by French Étienne Jacobet. It won't take much for Maï Olivier to open her storage room and show you a work commissioned by Ernest Weangaï or a catalog of one of her favorite artists. So much warmth and simplicity in the world of contemporary art fuels the pleasure of discovery....

MAISON EUROPÉENNE DE LA PHOTOGRAPHIE
5-7, rue de Fourcy, 4th arr., M° Saint-Paul, Pont-Marie
Tel: 01.44.78.75.00 – fax: 01.44.78.75.15 ▪ Open from 11 A.M. to 8 P.M.; closed Mondays, Tuesdays, and holidays – free admission on Wednesdays from 5 to 8 P.M. ▪

Opened in 1996, the Maison Européene de la Photographie holds major retrospectives and thematic exhibitions devoted entirely to photography. The group of artistic styles, from news and fashion photography to the vanguard of photography and plastic arts, have all found a place here in the thirteen thousand square feet of exhibition space. The reference library (close to twelve thousand books), the video library (monographs, interviews, films produced by photographer–video artists), the auditorium (with programs linked to the exhibits), the bookstore and café complete this "house for the ephemeral," as it was nicknamed by its president Henry Chapier.

MAX LINDER PANORAMA / Big screen
24, boulevard Poissonnière, 9th arr., M° Grands-Boulevards
Tel.: 01.40.30.30.31

One of the loveliest and most comfortable panoramic theaters in Paris, where the movies take on all their spectacular dimension. A great treat on a wintry Sunday morning is to cut short your lazing about in order to make it to the first showing around 11 A.M. (less crowded than in the afternoon) and settle snugly into one of the armchairs on the balcony to enjoy the show.

Chapter 5

MUSÉE JACQUEMART-ANDRÉ / *Former private mansion*
158, boulevard Haussmann, 8th arr., M° Miromesnil, Saint-Philippe-du-Roule
Tel.: 01.42.89.04.91 ▪ Open from 10 A.M. to 6 P.M. ▪

A spectacular folly in the very heart of Paris. Edouard André and his wife, passionate about art and travel, built this immense private mansion as a place to display their staggering collections. The French school from the eighteenth century, masterpieces from the Italian Renaissance, great Flemish masters—at every turn you'll be stunned by the wealth of works and the precision of their display. The opulence of the premises, the excess of the whole undertaking, the incredible density of artworks worthy of the greatest national museums is stupefying. If you're a bit taken aback by the splendor of it all, you can take a little break in the café. It's a small detail, but note that the ceiling was painted by Tiepolo.

MUSÉE PICASSO / *Chronological display*
5, rue de Thorigny, 3rd arr., M° Filles-du-Calvaire, Saint-Paul
Tel.: 01.42.71.25.21 ▪ Open from 9:30 A.M. to 5:30 P.M.; closed Tuesdays ▪

The most intelligent museum in Paris? From the blue period self-portrait to the *Vieil Homme Assis,* studies for *Les Demoiselles d'Avignon,* and *Le Baiser,* the exhibit unfolds as an enlightening chronology. Like breaks in text, parentheses punctuate your path, enriching it along the way: the artist's personal collection (drawings and paintings by Renoir, Cézanne, Matisse, Braque; African and Oceanic works of art), his links with writers, the sculpture garden, the ceramics…. In the heart of the Marais, within the pale stones of the very classic Hôtel de Salé, this is an illuminating stop.

NISSIM DE CAMONDO / *Eighteenth-century tribute*
63, rue de Monceau, 17th arr., M° Villiers
Tel.: 01.53.89.06.40

Inheritor of 63, rue de Monceau, the supremely wealthy Moïse de Camondo had it all destroyed in 1911 and ordered that it be rebuilt as a private mansion in the style of the Ancient Regime to harbor his collections of eighteenth-century objects. Less insane and of more human dimensions than the Jacquemart-André museum (see above), the project of this wealthy art lover is worthwhile mostly for the care brought to the arrangement of each pedestal table, vase, tapestry, and wing chair so that it contributes to the harmony of the group as a whole. The porcelain cabinet, an immense dresser holding services produced by Sèvres and Meissen, is a small museum in itself. Don't miss the luxurious kitchens, recently restored, that inspire cries of admiration.

PREMIÈRES LOGES / *Revise the classics*
15, rue Tiquetonne, 2nd arr., M° Étienne-Marcel, Les Halles
Tel.: 01.42.33.51.51

At the far end of a cobblestone courtyard, you'll discover a miniature workshop where you can find all the librettos—original versions and translations—of the season's musical performances. Opera buffs can enhance their pleasure by diving into a work's literary and musical analyses with commentaries on the different recordings, previous repertories, and act-by-act synopses. For neophytes, this place is a real asset—so as not to arrive for an evening at the Bastille feeling like a complete idiot...and for bluffing neighboring members of the audience with your erudition.

SENNELIER / *Everything for the painter*
3, quai Voltaire, 7th arr., M° Palais-Royal-Musée-du-Louvre
Tel.: 01.42.60.72.15

This Parisian institution is a wonderful color bazaar where you'll find all the paints and brushes you can imagine. The place that Beaux-Arts students go, you'll also run into creative types on Sundays who come in search of ocher powders to restore the shine to an old piece of furniture.

YVON LAMBERT / *New space*
108, rue Vieille-du-Temple, 3rd arr., M° Filles-du-Calvaire
Tel.: 01.42.71.09.33

There has recently been a major development in the life of this gallery (the first to exhibit Nan Goldin): Lambert has closed his small gallery dedicated to young talent located on the rue Vieille-du-Temple itself, and instead further developed his beautiful main space, situated off the street at the far end of a cobblestone courtyard. Artists who've never been exhibited before and more well-known names are now united. A perfect new setup for Yvon Lambert's favorites: Bertrand Lavier, Barbara Kruger, David Shrigley, Nielle Toroni, Jenny Holzer, Koo-Jeong-a…. A very active gallery in the promotion of contemporary art.

RUE LOUISE-WEISS / *Avant-garde magnet*
13th arr., M° Chevaleret

Mere mention of this street in the thirteenth arrondissement is something of an "open sesame" in the world of cultivated trendiness. It's impossible to frequent the small world of gallery openings and ignore this address representing the height of avant-garde. Although a bit sinister, this artery on the

Chapter 5

east edge of Paris now harbors a handful of galleries animating the artistic scene in Paris. We particularly recommend **Jennifer Flay** (at #20, tel: 01-44-06-73-60), **Emmanuel Perrotin** (#30, tel: 01-42-16-79-79), and **Almine Rech** (#24, tel: 01-45-83-71-90). Phone ahead to ensure that you don't end up there when the galleries are empty between exhibits.

Design]

For a long time, a piece of furniture or a lamp by Philippe Starck were the only concessions that French interiors made to design. With the arrival of new talent (Ronan Bouroulec, Matali Crasset, Jean-Marie Massaud) and the growing enthusiasm for postwar designers (Jean Prouvé, Charlotte Perriand), styles based less on cultural heritage have made headway in France. The French have learned to combine, create, and blend: a Chinese console with a Tsé & Tsé vase, a high-tech desk, bookshelves from the fifties.... From designers' boutiques to decor and unusual imported-goods shops, here are our suggestions so that you too can develop a passion for the beautiful and the unusual.

LES ARCHIVES DE LA PRESSE / *Fashion pages*
51, rue des Archives, 3rd arr., M° Rambuteau
Tel.: 01.42.72.63.93 – fax: 01.42.72.93.73

All the press from the 1800s to today has been stacked in the two floors of this incredible gallery. In the basement are the dailies, and the back issues of *Paris Match, Marie Claire, Elle, Point de Vue,* and television magazines. On the first floor—next to the sports, film, food, and travel sections—fashion dominates with issues of *Femina* from the thirties, reviews *(Vogue, Bazaar, L'Officiel, W),* and catalogs of yesterday and today, from *Chanel* to *Monoprix 2000.* A gold mine for journalists and especially designers, who come here to consult and pillage this extraordinary databank. Some leaf through the pages, others rent or buy copies; among the patrons are erudite collectors, the simply curious, and the obsessed. One can find happiness for as little as 65 francs (9,91 €), but count on around 300 francs (45,73 €) for historically important dates, and 6000 to 10 000 francs (914,69–1524,49 €) for rare items like Zola's famous article "*J'accuse….*"

CHEZ MAMAN / *Knoll attitude*
4, rue Tiquetonne, 2nd arr., M° Étienne-Marcel
Tel.: 01.40.28.46.09

A bit by chance, two charming Swiss women opened this shop specializing in furniture of the fifties and seventies, considered now to be the center of trendiness. On the first floor tables, chairs, armchairs, and white, orange, and green plastic lamps all contribute to the "psychedelic dollhouse" feel of the place. You gain access to the basement via a spiral staircase, where three small rooms are arranged with new arrivals. For fans of Charles Eames, Pierre Paulin, Arne Jacobson, Panton, and Knoll.

CHRISTOPHE DELCOURT / *Young generation*
76 *bis,* rue Vieille-du-Temple, 3rd arr., M° Temple, Hôtel-de-Ville
Tel.: 01.42.78.44.97

Noticed by Terence Conran, and now present in New York thanks to the latter's showroom, Christophe Delcourt belongs to the new young guard of French design. His dark walnut footstools and tables, rolling gray oak furniture, and modular metal lamps are simultaneously artistic and functional. Everything slides, curves, and rolls harmoniously for such massive and comfortable furniture of pure shapes. The gallery also opens its doors to other artists, ceramicists, textile manufacturers, and designers whose style is in keeping with that of their host.

DIAGONALE INDIGO / *Attic design*
52, rue des Martyrs, 9th arr., M° Saint-Georges
Tel.: 01.48.78.75.95

It's been ten years since Henry Pesah, an architect passionate about interior design and decoration, established his boutique/design agency at the center of the rue des Martyrs. In harmonious disorder in this modest space, you'll find superb objects signed by Alessi (coffee pots, kettles, platters, and accessories), Starck, and Tsé & Tsé (vases, garlands of lights); dozens of little design gifts starting at 100 francs (15,25 €) including Artemis and Flos lamps; the Accostage collection of curtains; furniture stamped by Driade and Zanotta; and a catalog of brands available for special order. A real design attic, Diagonale Indigo is also valuable for the electrical knowledge and enlightened suggestions of Henry Pesah. A nice stop on the way up the hill to Montmartre—at the risk of emerging wanting to remodel your entire apartment.

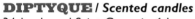

DIPTYQUE / *Scented candles*
34, boulevard Saint-Germain, 6th arr., M° Maubert-Mutualité
Tel.: 01.43.26.45.27

If for many foreigners Paris is—among other things—the capital of scented candles, Diptyque is an absolute must. Well before the vogue of room scents, this house—founded in the early sixties—maintained its links with the UK, from which it inherits, like all the major perfume brands, a terribly British flavor. Aligned on polished mahogany shelves, the bottles of eau de toilette, soaps, atomizers for interiors, potpourris, and scented candles exhaust the imagination with their infinite number of flowered, spiced, resinous, green,and woody perfumes.

ÉTAT DE SIÈGE / *1001 chairs*
1, quai de Conti, 1st arr., M° Pont-Neuf
Tel.: 01.43.29.31.60

Alternatively called "the seat in all its states." Two hundred and fifty styles on display—perched and nested chairs line the length of the walls like giant insects pinned by a crazy collector. There are some six thousand references in this store assiduously frequented by Beaux-Arts and Studio Berçot students. An object that's become rare in our day: about forty different models of stools are available here in wood, plastic, or metal; round or square; short-legged or super-high.

GALERIE FRANÇOIS LAFFANOUR DOWNTOWN /
Post-war designers
33, rue de Seine, 6th arr., M° Saint-Germain-des-Prés
Tel.: 01.46.33.82.41

In spring 2000, George Nelson's Coconut and Kangaroo chairs and Marshmallow couch will give way to the permanent furniture collections of post-war French architects. Original Corbusier, Charlotte Perriand, and Jean Prouvé pieces are stored in this minimalist gallery reminiscent of a family attic. Definitely one of Marc Jacobs' favorite addresses.

GALERIE JOUSSE SEGUIN / *3000 sq. ft. gallery*
5, rue des Taillandiers, 11th arr., M° Charonne, Bastille
Tel.: 01.47.00.32.35

Near their new-talents gallery on the rue de Charonne, Philippe Jousse and Patrick Séguin have opened a gallery over three thousand square feet in size devoted entirely to post-war architects and interior designers, where the works of Le Corbusier, Charlotte Perriand, Jean Prouvé, and Pierre Jeanneret are regularly exhibited. A very serious recommendation.

GALERIE SENTOU / *Objects for today*
24, rue du Pont-Louis-Philippe, 4th arr., M° Hôtel-de-Ville
Tel.: 01.42.71.00.01
26, boulevard Raspail, 7th arr., M° Vavin
Tel.: 01.45.45.49.00.05

The first to distribute Isamu Noguchi's paper lamps exclusively and then to welcome the highly-promoted Tsé & Tsé creations (garlands of lights and slim test-tube vases), the Galerie Sentou is today a necessary stop for young people on the road to domesticity. You'll also find Robert Le Heros' textiles, Migeon and Migeon's resins, and signed pieces by young designers like Arik Levy and Sori Yanagi.

JEAN-PHILIPPE DOUÉRIN / *Eclectic*
36, rue de Poitou, 3rd arr., M° Temple
Tel.: 01.42.77.69.57

Before opening his contemporary-furnishings boutique a year ago, Jean-Philippe Douérin worked in—among other things—floral decoration. Exhibited here are the fruits of his countless trips throughout Europe: Danish chairs, ceramics from Valauris, souvenirs from Asia. He has painstakingly restored all the furniture, and you'll find some real gems here—like glass light fixtures by Murano, Charles Eames chairs, and other fifties-era administrative furniture. Heterogeneous, but organized by theme like in a magazine (love, hacienda...), he likes to think of his selection as avant-garde, without a clear preference for one designer or another—unless it's perhaps a weakness for Jean Royère. His wish? To resist the temptation to become a showroom and to see a few more French people venture into his boutique.

KIRK ET ROSIE RICH / *Exoticism*
9, rue de la Trémoille, 8th arr., M° Alma-Marceau
Tel.: 01.47.23.81.00

With antique pink walls and polished black cement floors, Gisela Trigano and Alberto Pinto's new boutique looks like a volcanic beach at sunset. The decor is a fitting backdrop for the savvy display of goods pulled from the suitcases of these two globetrotters: lances from Papua New Guinea, pearl boxes in Balinese hues, a massive sculpted wood armchair from the Philippines, a Chinese lacquered console, antique textiles from Rajasthan, Nepalese jewelry.... The harmony stems from the refined style of the pieces—a mix of primitive art and contemporary design—be it a Murano vase or Pierre Lorenzo candlestick. All the objects are selected for their intrinsic beauty, rarity, or emotional impact. You'll also find beautiful travel books here.

MANUEL CANOVAS / *Precious fabrics*
5, rue de Furstenberg, 6th arr., M° Saint-Germain-des-Prés
Tel.: 01.43.26.89.31

One of the most interesting editors of interior textiles and painted papers has established himself in one of the most coveted places in Paris. Linen and cotton are his materials of choice, and the colors—some brilliant, in pink and blue; others muted, in tones of tobacco, slate, or leather—create woven or printed motifs inspired by distant horizons. The patterns of fans, flowers, leaves, and palm trees; the precision of the thread and lines; and the subtlety of the harmonies of color give these textiles the nobility and charm of vintage fabrics from abroad.

MARCHÉ SAINT-PIERRE / *Bargain textiles*
2, rue Charles-Nodier, 18th arr., M° Anvers
Tel.: 01.46.06.92.25

First there's the location: four floors equal in height to two of an office building, served by a freight-like elevator and run by an anachronistic operator. Then of course there are the fabrics: wool, gauze, cotton, silk, velvet that you buy by the meter (they unroll and sell between thirty and forty thousand every day) at exceptional prices, because they often come from the stock of big fashion houses just before inventory. Finally, there is the atmosphere, born from the mix of mothers, young couples, broke and sensible fashion victims, tourists on a spree, and savvy salespeople. A cliché of Paris at the foot of Sacré-Cœur.

NEOTU / *Window on Parisian design*
25, rue du Renard, 4th arr., M° Hôtel-de-Ville, Rambuteau
Tel.: 01.42.78.96.97 – fax: 01.42.78.26.27

Pierre Staudenmeyer was a marketing professor, Gerald Damon a computer consultant. The two friends developed an interest in the creation of contemporary furniture through a common interest in, of all things, psychoanalysis. A few steps from the Centre Georges-Pompidou in a vast two-story space, they exhibit, produce, and sell furniture, objects, and light fixtures by their favorite designers—Dan Friedman, Garouste and Bonetti, Sipek, Szekely— and guest designers. In France, the Neotu gallery is simultaneously the display window and obligatory stopover of an elitist, lively, and intentionally Baroque design style. The prices are, of course, quite high....

PRINTEMPS DESIGN / *Spacious showroom*
Centre Georges-Pompidou, 19, rue Beaubourg, 4th arr., M° Rambuteau
Tel.: 01.44.78.12.33

A new space designed by Renzo Piano—the architect of the Centre Georges-Pompidou—and dedicated to design is emerging in the heart of Paris across from the most recent Costes building. There is neither wall nor ceiling in this vast concrete mezzanine surrounded by metal guardrails and articulated around a central column of red and gray lacquered furniture punctuated by minimalist display windows. A modern, practical spirit and a mix of items—from 6 to 6000 francs (0,91–914,69 €), from old candy boxes to a wardrobe—reign in this anti-museum (no worship of objects here) and anti-Colette (no cult of trendiness). You are just as likely to run into design stars (Ingo Maurer, Philippe Starck) as the rising generation (Matal Crasset, Ronan and Erwan Bouroulec, Arik Levy)—a rare thing.

PUCES DE VANVES
14th arr., M° Porte-de-Vanves

Some people will tell you that it's at dawn, flashlight in hand, that you should explore the stands of the Vanves market in order to seek out your bargains. Others will tell you that, on the contrary, the best bargaining takes place around midday when the dealers, about to pack everything up, sell off their wares more readily. In either case, you'll love surveying their goods, which they spread out on tables with the self-contentment of happy magpies. Art

Deco lamps, Napoléon III dishware, embroidered linen pillowcases, fifties garden furniture, chinoiseries, objects from the attics of well-to-do families, vintage Hermès mackintoshes, silk kimonos.… Far from the well-scrubbed universe of Paris's select boutiques, here the worst items lie next to the finest—which is all part of the fun.

SHOWROOM CHRISTIAN LIAIGRE / *Ultra hip*
42, rue du Bac, 7th arr., M° Rue-du-Bac
Tel.: 01.53.63.33.66

If you want to get an idea of what Calvin Klein's Tribeca apartment or the seventy rooms of the very select Mercer hotel in New York look like, Christien Liaigre's showroom is the place to go. His generously proportioned furniture, with its pure lines and luxuriously dense materials, here attains the summit of simplicity and refinement. It's difficult to resist the deep settees, low tables polished like pebbles, and monasterial dark ebony benches which borrow their shapes from Zen minimalism and their materials from Africa or Polynesia. Valentino and Karl Lagerfeld—to mention only a few—are among the clients who have called upon the services of Paris's decorator of the moment. But beware: overexposure to Liaigre's style can provoke an allergy to gilding and other showy details.

THOMAS BOOG / *Chinoiseries*
36, passage Jouffroy, 9th arr., M° Richelieu-Drouot
Tel.: 01.47.70.98.10

You'll enter Thomas Boog's workshop, with its violet walls and muted lighting, as though walking into some kind of pagan chapel entirely dedicated to the cult of the seashell. But that which would make us flee from a seaside resort souvenir shop (mirrors, jewelry, candelabras, jewelry boxes, pedestals, vases—the entire lot encrusted with shells of all shapes and sizes), has a certain frosted delicacy and charm here. Pure geometric counterpoints, the Chinese lanterns soothe the eyes with their simple shapes and reassure us of the sanity of this designer who's back shop (not to be missed), entirely covered in limestone, creates the effect of an underwater cave for aquatic divinities.

Fashion]

Each season, the supremacy of Paris in matters of fashion is once again put under scrutiny. Has the eye of the hurricane passed on to New York or Milan? From one season to the next, however, the creativity of the Parisian designers continues to make the difference. Because you don't need this guide to make your way to the international designers along avenue Montaigne, we have presented a list of ambitious French designers that are rarely distributed abroad. From selective cutting-edge shops to made-to-measure boutiques, from trendy avant-garde to refined craftsmanship, we have designed the perfect circuit for fashion victims (female and male), informed of the latest trends certainly, but also open to new suggestions.

MULTIPLE LABELS

ABSINTHE / *Stylish bohemian*
74-76, rue Jean-Jacques-Rousseau, 1st arr., M° Les Halles
Tel.: 01.42.33.54.44

A far cry from the trends of minimalism and urban chic, Marthe Desmoulin's boutique favors young designers, often presenting limited series like those entirely based on vintage fabrics by stylist Christine Palmaccio. With leather armchairs, soft lighting, and an exuberant front window, this place shows a preference for a chic bohemian sort of femininity—and is fairly pricey. A wide selection of accessories, including Jamin Puech and Jacques Le Corre pieces, Alexandra François jewels, and shoes by Estelle Yomeda.

COLETTE / *Temple of trendiness*
213, rue Saint-Honoré, 1st arr., M° Tuileries
Tel.: 01.55.35.33.90

In two years, Colette has become an inescapable presence, upsetting the "geopolitics" by turning a chic neighborhood into a trendy one, and according to some, contributing to the revitalization of Parisian consumerism. Disparaged by critics as the "dictatorship of good taste," adulated by fashion victims, a case study for anthropologists and psychoanalysts in search of meaning, Colette is worth a visit. Basketball shoes, sportswear, cutting-edge designer electronics, and cosmetics share the first floor—resembling a museum with objects organized and labeled under glass. On the second floor, the current clothing trends are illustrated by a selection of designers, clear examples of the season's newest look. The temporary exhibits, CDs, books, and magazines occupy the mezzanines, the basement being reserved for a restaurant and bar selling every type of mineral water imaginable. On these three minimalist floors stalked by fashion editors, star watchers, addicts, the hip, and the stylish, one thing sums up the spirit of the place: an object's sell-by date logically depends entirely on how it sells. Everything must go....

LA DROGUERIE / *Feathers, sequins, etc.*
9, rue du Jour, 1st arr., M° Les Halles
Tel.: 01.45.08.93.27

Where can the chauffeur of a top model, an American couple staying at the Plaza, a grandmother in faded cross-stitch, a young girl in overalls, and a designer preparing for next season's collection all cross paths? At La

Droguerie. From the hooks of what was formerly a butcher shop in Les Halles now hang skeins of multicolored wool that, during the most recent shows in Paris, models were buying up to knit between struts down the catwalk. This family business founded in the seventies by four brothers and sisters offers the wildest and most hip selection of accessories and haberdashery imaginable. Brocaded braid; fabric petals and butterflies; infinite types of pearl, gold, and silver buttons; sequins; safety pins.…The mind reels as it tries to take in all the bowls' contents and the glistening displays in the windows. Beyond the poetry of the place, the practical side has not been lost on the fashion victims who stock up on sequins, pearl fringe, and feathers in an effort to give their old duds a new look or create cheap baubles.

L'ÉCLAIREUR / *Lifestyle*
3 *ter*, rue des Rosiers, 4th arr., M° Saint-Paul
Tel.: 01.48.87.10.22

It was during a stroll through Barney's that Armand Hadida came up with the idea to mix fashion, arts, and home in one shop scaled to human size. Modeled after the one on the Champs-Élysées, the shop on the rue des Rosiers benefits from a superb space, lit by glasswork dating back to 1900. Next to the plates designed by Fornasetti and the designer furniture, fashion designers "in gestation" rub shoulders with important role models like the influential Japanese and Belgian stylists. If you don't faint at the exorbitant prices, you might find a sheepskin coat by Neil Barett, a pair of slacks by Maharishi, or a metallic jacket by CP Company.

HOBBS / *Cashmere in all its forms*
45, rue Pierre-Charon, 8th arr., M° Franklin-Roosevelt
Tel.: 01.47.20.83.22

"Cashmere is like caviar: it exists in many forms." As well as having a good feel for the formula, Patrick Lipfchitz understands beautiful things. If your desire for cashmere doesn't take the form of a navy blue V-neck pullover, here is the boutique for you. Pullovers, reversibles, twin sets, cardigans, jackets, coats, scarves, jogging suits—cashmere exists in every form here and in every imaginable color (two thousand shades are available in the catalog!). If the style you're after doesn't exist, you can have it made-to-order, without an increase in price—count on paying about 600 francs (91,47 €) for a scarf alone, and around 2000 francs (304,90 €) for a turtleneck. In the fitting room, you'll run into show-biz stars as well as big-shot lawyers.

KABUKI / *The essentials and accessories*
21 and 25, rue Étienne-Marcel, 1st arr., M° Étienne-Marcel
Tel.: 01.42.33.55.65

Set on glass cubes or arranged in delicately lit alcoves, the shoes and accessories come first and take pride of place on the first floor of the two Kabuki shops. Women's styles are to be found at number 2—in a somewhat cold atmosphere of metal, polished wood, and cement interior—with a range of designers: Prada, Miu-Miu, Martine Sitbon, Helmut Lang, Sergio Rossi, Costume National, Patty Shelabarger…and of course, the Barbara Bui line (see p. 84). The husband of this designer—and president of the label—created the three Kabuki stores.

MARIA LUISA / *A cutting-edge selection*
2, rue Cambon, 1st arr., M° Concorde
Tel.: 01.47.03.96.15

Eponymous owner Marie Luisa is the source of the spirit and elegance of this multi-label shop. Far more private, and therefore even more chic than Colette, it's the Parisian point of reference for designer creations. You'll come for the collections of John Galliano, Martin Margiela, Véronique Leroy, Gaspard Yurkievitch, Helmut Lang, Hussein Chalayan; for the evening gowns of Nicolas Guesquières; for Balenciaga; and of course, for the Manolo Blahnik shoes.

ONWARD / *Modern trends*
147, boulevard Saint-Germain, 7th arr., M° Saint-Germain-des-Prés
Tel.: 01.55.42.77.55

Less conceptual and multidisciplinary than Colette, this recently refreshed, multiple-label boutique has become more refined, and now offers a more personal alternative to the temple of trendiness of the rue Saint-Honoré. Run by Christine Weiss for over twenty years, Onward doesn't specialize in any one key look, but offers instead a selection by the designers most in vogue at any given time. Loyal to Jean-Paul Gaultier and Martin Margiela since their early days, she proposes a distinctive selection of current European, Japanese, and American trends, neatly labeled with brief captions summarizing the style of each. Every season, the basement is entirely dedicated to the collection of one designer, who is also entrusted with its interior decoration for the occasion.

RAW ESSENTIALS / *Denim*
46, rue Étienne-Marcel, 2nd arr., M° Étienne-Marcel
Tel.: 01.42.21.44.33

French designer Pierre Morisset was based in Saint-Rémy-de-Provence with Dutch label G-Star before suddenly becoming the darling of a generation lost to Levi's, who now find all the styles and denim they could want here in his boutique. Unbleached cloth—teased, mechanically woven, and imported from Japan; small sizes or a skin-tight look; four different leg lengths: this is the kingdom of trendy blue jeans. If the legend is true, Madonna stopped here just before Calvin Klein himself arrived to try on a few things. More often though, you might run into French rapper MC Solaar or football star Zinedine Zidane.

LES TROIS MARCHES / *Antique fashions*
1, rue Guisarde, 6th arr., M° Saint-Germain-des-Prés
Tel.: 01.43.54.74.18

Behind a facade resembling a village dry-goods shop, one hundred square feet are devoted to the vintage cult of Hermès and Chanel. You never inherited that Kelly or padded Chanel bag of your dreams? To quench this unsatisfied fantasy, head off to Catherine B., not your shrink. This enthusiastic antique fashion dealer has been buying these two brands for years now, and can even be asked to look for that rare pearl you've always wished for if you don't find what you want in her miniature studio.

DESIGNERS

APC / *A sure bet*
Flagship store: 3, rue de Fleurus, 6th arr., M° Rennes
Tel.: 01.42.22.12.77

Tweed, suede, flannel, and discretion are the principal characteristics of APC's style (Atelier de Production et de Création, or Studio of Production and Creation); but it's for the impeccably cut unbleached denim that one frequents this main store so assiduously. "My APC, your APC, our APC": the store's acronym has found its place in the dictionary of fashion victims. But it goes without saying that it isn't proper to ask someone if they're wearing APC jeans. You just know....

AZZEDINE ALAÏA / *Ultra feminine*
6, rue de Moussy, 4th arr., M° Hôtel-de-Ville
Tel. : 01.42.72.19.19

The stylized name of the designer is barely visible, engraved above the door under the facade of frosted glass panes. No sign marks the place—where you must buzz to enter. The store, located in a vast concrete and red brick warehouse and decorated in the designer's style, is one of the most discreet and striking stores in the city. The proportions of the fitting rooms, decorated with two immense vintage mirrors, are those of a boutique, and the collection—sober and sexy—seems to float on disparate racks designed by Julian Schnabel. Like Hitchcock's fleeting presence on screen, Alaïa's harried silhouette can occasionally be seen hidden behind the window of his studio on the mezzanine.

BARBARA BUI / *Impecable style*
43, rue des Francs-Bourgeois, 4th arr., M° Saint-Paul
Tel. : 01.53.01.88.05
23, rue Étienne-Marcel, 1st arr., M° Étienne-Marcel
Tel. : 01.40.26.43.65
50, avenue Montaigne, 8th arr., M° Champs-Élysées-Clemenceau
Tel. : 01.42.25.05.25

A Barbara Bui café (27, rue Étienne-Marcel), a new address on the right bank on the avenue Montaigne, store openings in New York and Milan: this designer is cutting a wide swath with her signature soft-tech style presented on smooth concrete counters. Featherweight nylon slacks; zipped jackets; progressive-looking gabardine trench coats; shrink-wrapped silk and Lycra T-shirts from the Initials collection in black, white, gray, beige, purple, and navy blue dominate the two lines of this new name for the chic, urban, thirty-something set.

CHRISTOPHE LEMAIRE / *Sophisticated casual*
36, rue de Sévigné, 3rd arr., M° Saint-Paul
Tel. : 01.42.74.54.90

Putty-colored ceilings, pale acid-yellow lacquered racks, fitting rooms hung with tatamis, small sitting room windows that open onto a cobblestone courtyard: Christophe Lemaire's first shop reflects his refined and graphic all-cotton, easy-wear style. We like his sexy and fragile unlined skirts, his little woven and fine poplin tops, his details—exposed seams, turned-back sleeves.... A serene, almost austere little spot in a universe of sometimes hysterical fashions; unfortunately inflation ruthlessly affected his most recent collection.

Chapter 7

ÉRIC BERGÈRE / *Allure*
16, rue de la Sourdière, 1st arr., M° Tuileries
Tel.: 01.47.03.33.19

This showroom at the rue de la Sourdière should become the designer's premier Parisian shop come June 2000. We impatiently await the chance to find the unisex suits; fitted frock coats; long, fluid jackets and short dandy ones; safari jackets, smocks, carpenter's coats, and race car jackets made from jersey; and cotton gabardine, viscose canvas, and other supple fabrics that the designer works into fluid and flattering silhouettes.

EROTOKRITOS / *Designers to keep tabs on*
58, rue d'Argout, 2nd arr., M° Sentier
Tel.: 01.42.21.44.60

As unlikely as it may seem, Erotokritos is the real name of this former assistant to Martine Sitbon. The secret to the clothes he designs with Austrian stylist Rudolph Ritzer is that you must try them on to fully experience their ingenuity and hyper-femininity. This little bustier made of netting and cotton dangling from its hanger, that little iridescent mesh pullover...reveal themselves to be exquisitely becoming once they're on. A combination of dreamy fantasy and great structural soundness, the entire line is the fruit of a slightly schizophrenic collaboration with romantic yet comfortable results. A real designer's line with a ceiling of around 1000 francs (152,45 €) for the most expensive items.

ISABEL MARANT / *Wise blends*
1, rue Jacob, 6th arr., M° Saint-Germain-des-Prés
Tel.: 01.43.26.25.91
16, rue de Charonne, 11th arr., M° Charonne
Tel.: 01.49.29.71.55

"Commercial, realistic, and creative" is how this leader of young French designers sums up the spirit and success of her collections. Feminine with a touch of glamour (long skirts cut on a diagonal, drawstring or Empire-style low-cut blouses, feather and fur details), her line is not revolutionary, but intelligently mixes cosmopolitan culture with contemporary trends. Essentially the perfect store for an impulse buy, when you "ab-so-lu-te-ly" need a little something for tonight, or simply need to lift your spirits....

JEAN-PAUL GAULTIER / *The king of fashion*
6, rue Vivienne, 1st arr., M° Palais-Royal
Tel.: 01.42.86.05.05

With Yves Saint Laurent as "ultimate master," Hermès as a partner, and the press as an adoring mirror, the former *enfant terrible* of French fashion has come a long way. His smock, his new look by Yvette Horner, and his costume designs with pointed breasts for Madonna will be part of France's heritage from now on. Jean-Paul Gaultier still cultivates his own form of eccentricity and set design in his neo-futuristic gallery, where one fully penetrates his universe, pierced with portholes in a seafaring spirit. Unfortunately, the haute couture collections are missing—shown by appointment only.

JÉRÔME L'HUILLIER / *Cocktail-party chic*
138-139, galerie de Valois, Palais-Royal, 1st arr., M° Palais-Royal
Tel.: 01.49.26.07.07

Very much inspired by the film world, Jérôme Huillier's style could be subtitled "In search of lost glamour." With a cocktail-party spirit—all in silk, mesh, and crepe, and printed in brilliant colors—his sheath dresses and skirts are something of a cross between a chic cruise and an embassy reception. Somewhat in danger of falling into obsolescence from trying to maintain an outdated vision of femininity, but deliciously precious.

MARITHÉ ET FRANÇOIS GIRBAUD / *With the times*
38, rue Étienne-Marcel, 2nd arr., M° Étienne-Marcel
Tel.: 01.53.40.74.20

Pioneers in synthetics and cutting-edge fabrics, this duo has made a remarkable comeback to the Parisian fashion scene. More closely resembling the NASA research labs than a design studio, their clothes are made with ceramic materials, laser-cut or welded seams, sub-sonic knits, zips, pleats, reversible and thermal fibers. Their latest store, five thousand square feet in a duplex on the rue Étienne-Marcel, is entirely dedicated to the Stealth Concept. Inspired by the performances and aesthetic of the aviation combat stealth F117, this tongue-in-cheek military wardrobe is designed to dress the "soldiers of peace" for the twenty-first century, who care more about "being" than "seeming." We are just happy to find the baggy outfits with lots of pockets that we like best for vacations.

MARONGIU / *Hip chic*
203, rue Saint-Honoré, 1st arr., M° Tuileries
Tel.: 01.49.27.96.38

Two steps from Colette, it is hard to imagine anything more hip for a first store, especially since it is so light and bare. Asymmetry; exaggeration of sizes; plenty of mesh, Lycra, and metallic chiffon for dresses that sway when you twirl; long gathered skirts and narrow suits. In the ten years that he has been dressing women, Marongiu has affirmed his style and made his mark, and even today has fun designing dishware lines. Lovers of fashion are swooning—we are a bit more reserved, as the prices here are very dissuasive.

MARTINE SITBON / *Perfect shapes*
13, rue de Grenelle, 7th arr., M° Sèvres-Babylone
Tel.: 01.44.39.84.44

One of the rare female designers to be ranked among today's great fashion gurus, Martine Sitbon has set up shop in an old printing house. The deep space opens like a funnel from the cramped entryway toward the back of the shop, lit up by a multi-colored Plexiglas wall. At the end, a staircase that leads nowhere—the second floor does not exist. With red tones, plum-colored couches, and white walls, the setting is reminiscent of a chapel's fervent hues. Martine Sitbon has fans—and many of them. Cut velvet, androgynous yet fluid shapes are her trademark style—admirable for their irreproachable details, their fitted but not-too-tight silhouettes, their absolute elegance somewhat inclined toward a masculine look. Very high-end design, as the price tags eloquently reveal.

MERCERIE D'UN SOIR / *Idiosyncratic textiles*
37, rue de Grenelle, 7th arr., M° Sèvres-Babylone
Tel.: 01.45.48.26.13

This organdy dress? Made from oil filters. That black, raw-silk evening coat? It's made of photo filters. After tree bark, ceramic, mail bags, and multi-colored woven plastic threads, Étienne Brumel is now in her paper phase. This unusual designer dresses all of Paris with recycled materials that she transforms into filmy and sexy outfits fit for a princess. Passionate and extraordinary, she focuses on her recipes for giving the impression of a flat stomach, but she can also lift a bosom, align a waist, or erase a roundness in the hips with the simple magic of her tailoring.

XULY BET / *Hot couture*
5, forum des Halles, porte Berger, 1st arr., M° Les Halles
Tel.: 01.42.33.47.50

The pope of hot design, king of recycling, and leader of street fashion, Xuly Bet—copied a thousand times—has evolved toward a more sophisticated style without losing his originality or his freshness. Intentionally tight fitting, between ethnic motif and urban jungle, his style is that of a generation raised in the eighties. At the center of the Designer Space of Les Halles (a vast underground mall in the center of Paris), his boutique is the only one to carry a real name and worth going out of your way for.

JAPANESE DESIGNERS

COMME DES GARÇONS / *Avant-garde*
42, rue Étienne-Marcel, 2nd arr., M° Étienne-Marcel
Tel.: 01.42.33.05.21

At Comme des Garçons—where any good practicing fashion victim must go on a pilgrimage—Rei Kawakubo and Junya Watanabe's collaborative line keeps your attention because of its inventive academicism and gracious silhouettes, its nod to the Dior style of the fifties, and its very specialized research into the uses of revolutionary fabrics like those in its poetic spring/summer 2000 collection.

ISSEY MIYAKE / *Perfect elegance*
3, place des Vosges, 4th arr., M° Saint-Paul, Bastille
Tel.: 01.48.87.01.86

Haute-couture details, variations on classic cuts, inventions of new shapes, a wealth of fabrics. This Japanese designer's outfits have two sides—one diurnal, one nocturnal—and are therefore always in exactly the same tone regardless of the hour or the circumstances: the very definition of elegance perfectly achieved. Beneath the arches of the place des Vosges, this is one of Paris's loveliest boutiques. Grace Jones once closed it to try clothes on in peace, transforming it into one giant fitting room.

TSUMORI CHISATO / *Urban outfits*
20, rue Barbette, 3rd arr., M° Saint-Paul, Hôtel-de-Ville
Tel.: 01.42.78.18.88

Cross the Marais for this thematic stroll on the trail of Tsumori Chisato—one of Issey Miyake's former assistants. She is newly established in a Paris shop entirely designed by architect–designer Christian Biecher. Cement resin, sheets of aluminum, glass fibers, and ash wood: the materials of this Spartan "studio" make for a rather harsh setting where the clothes are mere stains of black, white, and orange—futurist uniforms for protection from the elements.

YOHJI YAMAMOTO / *Timeless*
47, rue Étienne-Marcel, 1st arr., M° Étienne-Marcel
Tel.: 01.45.08.82.45

To stroll back up to the place des Victoires and wander along the rue Étienne-Marcel—where Yohji Yamamoto and Comme des Garçons are almost face-to-face—is a reminder of their stunning synchronized début on the Parisian fashion scene in 1981. At Yamamoto's, asymmetry and black and white make for a semi-austere, semi-wild style—something of a cross between school uniforms and tramps' rags. We would give a great deal for one of these ample coats or sweaters whose oversized sleeves fold back at the wrists.

ZUCCA / *Life's colors*
8, rue Saint-Roch, 1st arr., M° Tuileries
Tel.: 01.44.58.98.88

To finish this Japanese stroll, push on toward the Tuileries to have a look at Zucca, a few steps from Colette. The designer's new playground—a vast, airy and Zen ambulatory—offers menswear for the first time. And of course, handsome oversized silicon watches, fluorescent nylon shopping bags, and the Zucca Work line (Zucca Travail).

MENSWEAR

JOSÉ LÉVY / *Masculine coquetry*
70, rue Vieille-du-Temple, 3rd arr., M° Saint-Paul, Hôtel-de-Ville
Tel.: 01.48.04.39.16

A "Parisian bad boy" style—half-cocky, half-poser—that doesn't mind borrowing a few mixed signals from women's fashion, like the tongue-in-cheek tuxedo pants lined with a braid of satin at the ankle and sold with extra matching ribbon.

KABUKI / *Total look*
23, rue Étienne-Marcel, 1st arr., M° Étienne-Marcel
Tel.: 01.42.33.13.44

Opened in September 1999, when all the Parisian department stores were refreshing, refreshing, and expanding their menswear departments, the new Kabuki space dedicated to menswear fills a gap—just like its feminine counterpart (see p. 82). In six thousand square feet punctuated by metal and glass is the entire panoply of the trendy man: Prada, Prada Sport, Miu-Miu, Helmut Lang, Martine Sitbon, Calvin Klein.

LAGERFELD GALLERY / *Exclusively Karl*
40, rue de Seine, 6th arr., M° Saint-Germain-des-Prés
Tel.: 01.55.42.75.51

Set apart in the geography of Paris—somewhere between mausoleum, art gallery, and fashion boutique. In one thousand square feet designed by Andrée Putman, Mr. Lagerfeld actually displays items from his personal universe—photos, perfumes, books, magazines—that, if they don't cover the designer's entire career, certainly sketch out an esthetically pleasing (and somewhat morbid) atmosphere. In the basement, reached by a magnificent slate staircase, his signature women's and men's ready-to-wear lines are on display, as well as accessories, including those designed for Fendi. In addition, Karl Lagerfeld had long hoped to open a bookstore specializing in contemporary art, which he accomplished with the creation of **7L Librairie** (7, rue de Lille, 7th arr., M° Rue-du-Bac, Saint-Germain-des-Prés, tel: 01-42-92-03-58). Architecture, design, land art, photography, fashion, artists' books, and poetry are the seven principal themes featured in this space—designed with a rough concrete floor and inviting minimalist layout. You can touch, look, and stroll peacefully, with the delicious feeling that you have entered someone's rich private library.

MARIA LUISA / *Menswear designers*
38, rue du Mont-Thabor, 1st arr., M° Concorde
Tel.: 01.42.60.89.33

The men's version of the women's boutique (see p. 82): Tomas Maler, Timothy Everest, Clements Ribiero, Martin Margiela, Martine Sitbon, Samsonite, Smedley.

PANOPLIE / *Eclectic selection*
7, rue d'Argout, 2nd arr., M° Sentier
Tel.: 01.40.28.90.35

At the end of a courtyard, this specialized shop is intentionally hidden to allow it to select its clientele, aged 17 to 77 years old. Its philosophy is distinguished on the one hand by a love for beautiful details tinted with nostalgia—designers like Xavier Delcour, Ann Demeulemeester, Kostas Mukudis, Martine Sitbon, Ato, Vivienne Westwood, John Smedley's sweaters; on the other by high-tech clothing and down jackets that turn into bulletproof parkas—signed by Samsonite, Mandarina Duck, Final Home, Skim Come, Vexed Generation....

YVES SAINT LAURENT / *New elegance*
12, place Saint-Sulpice, 6th arr., M° Saint-Sulpice
Tel.: 01.43.26.84.40

Close to thirty years after its inauguration in 1971, the men's YSL boutique has been renovated by Richard Gluckman. A black tile floor, luminous wall, stainless steel displays, aluminum furnishings, spacious black tent cabins sheltering screens: the recreated space—a sort of futurist transition zone—corresponds perfectly with the redefinition of his signature look and the menswear collection, directed by Hedi Slimane, who's been in charge of the ready-to-wear line since the summer of 1996. A contemporary intersection of fashion and art, the boutique regularly exhibits the work of artists such as Craig Kalpakjian.

ACCESSORIES

AFTER / *End-of-series shoes*
13, rue de Turbigo, 2nd arr., M° Étienne-Marcel
Tel.: 01.42.36.44.34

A cross between a multiple-label and vintage boutique, this ultimate extension of the Kabuki stores (see pp. 82 and 90) presents current collections and past series of the big names in shoes: Michel Perry, Rodolphe, Menudier, Sergio Rossi, Dries van Noten, Prada.... Even if we're still in the same family, we have left behind the frigid atmosphere of the Kabuki universe with a checkered marble floor and curved furnishings created by Pucci di Rossi, for a sales concept worth watching.

BIONDINI / *Imelda Marcos's dream stop*
Galerie 26, 26, avenue des Champs-Élysées, 8th arr., M° Champs-Élysées-Clemenceau
Tel.: 01.45.62.14.40

The first multiple-label boutique entirely devoted to shoes, Biondini is for the Imelda Marcos in each of us. A mosaic-tile floor, forged metal shelves, golden lighting—all is done to glorify the inventive, sophisticated, urban shoe. You'll find large sizes here (Robert Clergerie, Charles Jourdain, Michel Perry), Italian labels (Vicini, Pollini, Casadeï), the fashion designers (Karl Lagerfeld, Christian Lacroix), and the newcomers on the scene (Rodolphe Menudler, Pierre Hardy, Alain Tondowsky). Refined low-front shoes, sculpted boots, sexy mules, strappy sandals, designer tennis shoes—it's impossible not to find happiness here.

LE CACHEMÉRIEN / *The must of cashmere*
12, rue de l'Échaudé, 6th arr., M° Saint-Germain-des-Prés
Tel.: 01.43.29.93.32

If you managed to bypass the overdose of pashmina shawls made in bulk and sold by the yard, stop by *the* cashmere boutique of Paris. The woman in charge, an Italian married to a Kashmirian, will explain to you the time-consuming craft work in India that goes into creating each of the patterns available in her boutique: gossamer scarves woven—and sometimes embroidered—by hand, applying ancestral methods to a contemporary style. For 5000 francs (762,25 €), you will be able to leave draped like a sultana in a unique and sumptuous piece, but you will also be able to find happiness for under 1000 francs (152,45 €), whether you fall for a merino-silk-blend muffler for 800 francs (122 €) or an acid-colored organza veil at 300 francs (45,73 €). And because a spirit of elegant courtesy reigns here, you are welcome to inquire at length and leave without a thing.

JAMIN PUECH / *Mischevious bags*

61, rue d'Hauteville, 10th arr., M° Poissonnière
Tel.: 01.40.22.08.32

In 1992, the Bergdorf Goodman department store presented and distributed bags by Benoît Jamin and Isabelle Puech for the first time. Since then, between two collections created for the runways of Chloé and Karl Lagerfeld, the duo has created its own boutique where the carcass of a tattered old Empire couch rests imposingly—an old fetish from their early days. From the small evening purse brocaded with pearls to the sober leather shopping tote, their bags—with perfect finishing touches—are

Chapter 7

offered with humor and elegance at a very reasonable range of prices. Although quite a way from the chic and trendy neighborhoods, their shop is really worth a trip.

LEE YOUNG HEE / *Zen house linens*
109, rue du Bac, 7th arr., M° Sèvres-Babylone
Tel.: 01.42.84.24.84

One of the most exotic and refined boutiques in the city—modeled after a teahouse on water—is reached by crossing a footbridge along which a display window houses sumptuous pendants, small sharkskin cases, and lovely evening bags. In the basement, reached by a fan-shaped staircase, an exquisite line of delicate and fresh household linens and indoor clothing made of silk and linen are for sale exclusively—that we prefer even over this Korean designer's ready-to-wear line.

MICHEL PERRY / *Sexy shoes*
4, rue des Petits-Pères, 2nd arr., M° Bourse
Tel.: 01.42.44.10.07

Skillfully renovated by architect Gregory Raballand, this shoe designer's upscale boutique is draped with orange and pink curtains like a modern boudoir for "Venetian punks." It's terribly chic and at the very extreme limit of bad taste, and therefore underscores the classicism of the creator's shoes perfectly. At the center of this intimate space, a large black leather ottoman invites you to try on the form-fitting boots and arched low-front shoes tucked into alcoves in the wall, just as you'd take a seat on the bench in a museum hall to better contemplate the canvases on the wall.

SILKIE / *Painted silk*
43, rue des Francs-Bourgeois, 4th arr., M° Saint-Paul
Tel.: 01.40.27.84.49

Sylvette Caroll, painter of fabrics, opened her boutique in the Marais in 1999. In a lovely setting of warm wood tones and luminous transparency, you'll have a seat in one of the comfortable nineteenth-century Chinese-style armchairs to better choose between the pastel-toned taffeta shawls (straight-edged or bordered with ostrich plumes), the organza scarves whose painted images look like trompe-l'oeil embroidery, the thirties-era sequined organdy chokers.... With fans and painted silk stockings for sale as well, it all exudes an antiquated spirit of coquetry that the creator hopes women will develop a taste for again. Each piece is unique and can be made-to-order to go with a specific outfit. A very affordable selection of impulse items—ceramic boxes that you would think were made of sharkskin, Galimard perfume spray bottles found exclusively in Paris, jewelry—complete this universe situated somewhere between traditional and contemporary art.

STELLA CADENTE / *The Lolita touch*
22, rue de Grenelle, 7th arr., M° Sèvres-Babylone
Tel.: 01.45.44.89.89

A store that evokes the spirit of a dollhouse and revives little-girl fantasies for simple, little, featherweight jewels reminiscent of fairy tales and princesses. The designer is also developing a delicate ready-to-wear line: little embroidered sweaters, felt skirts, pastel woolens. It's a paradise of playful femininity, far from the world of the businesswoman. Ideal for special events—a friend's wedding, a candlelit dinner—and small budgets.

SWAROVSKI / *Jeweled bags*
7, rue Royale, 8th arr., M° Concorde
Tel.: 01.40.17.07.40

Ten years ago, Karl Lagerfeld's former collaborator Rose-Marie Le Gallais had an inkling that women would start paying more attention to their accessories. It is she that directed the world leader in cut crystal toward her precious bags. Glazed lambskin; chiffon; satin adorned with glittering crystalline pearls; limestone, gold, and silver—an extraordinarily refined union of fine leather goods and high-end jewelry. Just the accessory to spruce up that little black dress.

WALTER STEIGER / *Ergonomics*
83, rue du Faubourg-Saint-Honoré, 8th arr., M° Saint-Philippe-du-Roule
Tel.: 01.42.66.65.08

The Swiss boot maker will tell you himself: he is not obsessive and he works to make shoes for women who walk. This statement has meant that since his early days (he introduced Lycra into the world of shoes) he has done research in both esthetics and ergonomics. His shoes—beautiful and comfortable—and his felt ankle boots, ballerina slippers, and loafers—low-heeled or with molded soles—are therefore ideal for going out and conquering the city. No matter who you are, smiling and professional salespeople will help you out.

LINGERIE
FIFI CHACHNIL / *Funny and sexy*
26, rue Cambon, 8th arr., M° Concorde
Tel.: 01.42.60.38.86

A prestigious new address for Fifi Chachnil, who has set up shop right across the street from the main Chanel store on rue Cambon. Ultra-kitsch, Fifi Chachnil's boutique, with its tulle curtains and pink satin couch, is a humorous variation on a harlot's lair. *Fifi* is the diminutive for Delphine Véron, the very trendy designer of this line of light and sweet lingerie. The pastels are lovely and the prices mild for the panties, brassieres, and combinations in silk lace or nylon that flutter under your skirt.

SABBIA ROSA / *Silk underclothes*
73, rue des Saints-Pères, 6th arr., M° Saint-Germain-des Prés
Tel.: 01.45.48.88.37

The boutique looks like a young girl's dressing room—but carries lingerie for the *femme fatale*. Sabbia Rosa has never heard of any fabrics other than silk and lace. When running our fingers over these fabulous negligées, we dream of how great they'd look warmed up with a little sweater—in cashmere of course—so as to be able to wear them out in broad daylight.

JEWELRY
BARBOZA / *Charming gems*
356, rue Saint-Honoré, 1st arr., M° Tuileries
Tel.: 01.42.60.67.08

It's just a tiny workshop a few steps from the place Vendôme, but its reputation is known across the Atlantic. You can buy and sell charms, antique pieces, or compositions here, all under the icy blue eyes of Madame Gribe. Although a bit daunting the first time around, she will let herself be subdued and does not hesitate when faced with a difficult and delicate repair. "I do impossible things," she says, smiling and admitting that she's been defeated "once a decade."

DINH VAN / *Designer jewelry*
16, rue de la Paix, 2nd arr., M° Opéra
Tel.: 01.42.61.74.49

Without a doubt one of the most unusual jewelers of the place Vendôme. Of Vietnamese origin and in Paris since 1976, Jean Dinh Van has revolutionized the world of gems by working to make jewelry less sacred. Rather than follow the tradition of complexly precious designs, he chose instead to impose the sober design of refined geometric forms. All ivory and coral, brightened up by a few touches of fuchsia, his new boutique isn't intimidating—something we particularly appreciate in this neighborhood.

FABIEN DE MONTJOYE / *Baroque settings*
177, rue Saint-Honoré, 1st arr., M° Palais-Royal
Tel.: 01.42.60.14.12

A leisurely, gentlemanly, old-world setting reigns in the little office of this provincial aristocrat. We listen to him with pleasure as he tells us of his gems, much as one would relate news of a family friend. The unique cameos, pearls, and rhinestones of his jewels and the reasonable prices make for an extravagant curiosity shop packed with history—and often humor as well. An excellent place to treat yourself to a luxurious pair of bohemian earrings and invent a fine heritage for yourself.

VINTAGE AND SECOND-HAND

ANOUSCHKA / *A century of fashion*
6, avenue du Coq, 9th arr., M° Trinité
Tel.: 01.48.74.37.00

A former model who's just crazy about clothes, Anouschka travels the world, from deep in the Auvergne to the fringes of India, to re-supply a stock of hundreds of shoes, dresses, skirts, coats, suits, nighties, raincoats, men's suits, and accessories that date from the twenties up through the eighties. Hanging racks three rows high surround the four rooms of this superb pre-Haussmann apartment. Anouschka doesn't live here of course, but she's in charge of the premises. According to her, few private clients venture into this insane dressing room, discouraged by the crammed racks of hangers and the sheer volume of clothing. This passionate shopowner opens her doors to the staff of the fashion houses and design studios in search of inspiration. A few models also come here to unearth vintage outfits. By appointment only.

DIDIER LUDOT / *Designer vintage*
125, galerie de Valois, jardins du Palais-Royal, 1st arr., M° Palais-Royal
Tel.: 01.40.15.01.04

Didier Ludot puts all his haute-couture expertise and talent into selecting timeless vintage outfits whose chic is not outdated by so much as a wrinkle. His new workshop, maintained by the quasi-twin of fashion critic

Suzy Menkes, has applied this theory to the famous little black dress—the Holy Grail eternally sought by elegant women everywhere. Signed by Balenciaga, Yves Saint Laurent, Christian Dior, Yohji Yamamoto, Jacques Fath, and Chanel, the styles in his selection offer countless exquisite variations on this inexhaustible theme.

FRIPE'N STARS SON & IMAGE / *Vintage and leather*
8, rue Sainte-Croix-de-la-Bretonnerie, 3rd arr., M° Hôtel-de-Ville
Tel.: 01.42.76.03.72

Simon mans the cash register and the stock of this second-hand clothing shop that stays open well after office hours. He explains the rules of the game to you with confidence and with a touch of provocation: some pieces (seventies-era embroidered suede coats and leather jackets) are not priced according to what they're worth. Setting up great surprises for clientele willing to plunge full swing into the strata of rags is one of his great joys. And you will be grateful to him when he cedes to you without a word of protest that handsome beige astrakhan coat with its lining in impeccable shape for under 500 francs (76,22 €). "It's all part of the game," he'll tell you, smiling.

GUERRISOL / *From 10 francs and up*
31-33, avenue de Clichy, 17th arr., M° Place-de-Clichy
Tel.: 01.53.42.31.31

Guerrisol is a legend. Tangled at the bottom of crates and heaped on bulging racks, marvels are certain to be found in this vintage-clothing shop: satin dresses, little floral blouses, short and fitted jackets straight from the fifties and sixties—the period from which Prada, Miu-Miu, Gucci, and other houses find inspiration. The point in shopping here being obviously that the low-waisted Yamamoto-style pants cost between 10 and 50 francs (1,52–7,62 €). This miracle has a rational explanation: stocked by the cubic meter from warehouses in the suburbs, before arriving in the boutique the clothes are submitted to the severe screening of a freelance designer hired by the shop to select pieces that fit with the spirit of the times. If the trend is toward hippie chic, count on regular arrivals of fringed coats, low-cut, drawstring tunics, and flounced skirts.

BEAUTY

Beauty]

Where can you get a massage under a Berber tent, savor the benefits of thalasso therapy only a metro stop away, or find a bottle of *Tuberose criminelle* perfume or a glass of vitamin-enriched wheat grass juice? Do you know that you need to make an appointment three weeks ahead for a hair colorist or a Chinese pedicure? Since you might feel like changing your look, might be dreaming of a seaweed wrap or—for the gentlemen—an old-fashioned shave (even if you're only here a few days), here is a selection of addresses...a deluxe makeup bag of sorts.

ANNE SÉMONIN / *Massage under a Berber tent*
108, rue du Faubourg-Saint-Honoré, 8th arr., M° Saint-Philippe-du-Roule
Tel.: 01.42.66.24.22

Two doors down from the Bristol hotel, this salon offers a wide range of beauty care and easy appointments, despite the tight quarters. The credo of the salon, created by Anne Semonin, high priestess of customized aroma-therapy and successful businesswoman: specific beauty treatments for each skin type. You'll give a few answers on your life, work, favorite foods, ten-dencies, and concerns; then plants, trace elements, and minerals are blended in front of you for a healing cure. Three discreet and efficient estheticians also offer the special "jet lag" treatment. Reserved for backs aching from interminable trips, a volcanic mudpack is applied to the tired vertebrae, where it tingles, heats, and awakens your stiff muscles. Miraculous, we promise you; pleasant, so they say. In the basement, in a shadowy room reminiscent of a Berber tent—draped in beige cotton and with palm-leaf mats and an open stove—a masseuse exercises her art. Energetic drainage (Tuesdays and Saturdays), plantar reflexology (Mondays, Wednesdays, and Thursdays), shiatsu and Thai massages (Mondays, Wednesdays, and Thursdays). For a facial and a "jet lag" treatment, allow about an hour and a half and around 800 francs (121,96 €).

ATELIER DE BEAUTÉ ANNE SÉMONIN / *For Men*
Espace Madelios, 23, boulevard de la Madeleine, 8th arr., M° Madeleine
Tel.: 01.53.45.00.31

The men's version of the beauty studio mentioned above, where gentle-men can taste a wheat-germ cocktail (hazelnut flavored) for free at the Herb Bar counter.

BAINS DU MARAIS / *Baths*
31, rue des Blancs-Manteaux, 4th arr., M° Hôtel-de-Ville
Tel.: 01.44.61.02.02

The creators of this establishment resolved the painful dilemma of vivacious Parisians who perspire heavily yet are smitten with hygiene. The Bains du Marais well deserve their reputation for a clinical level of cleanliness. Happily, the place, situated between the Roman thermal baths and the *hammam* (steam baths), is full of charm as well—the impeccable cleanliness of a shrink-wrapped bathrobe and towel and the thoughtful detail of a blue cot-ton *pareo* for you to knot around your hips. The refined decor of the marble and beige sandstone, soft light of the small lanterns smelling of eucalyptus, thick curls of hot steam, and hum of secrets relayed in hushed tones: is there any better way to do nothing and lose all sense of time? If you've made an appointment, you can pull yourself out of your delicious stupor with an exfoliation and vigorous massage, a somewhat toned-down version of the one the masseuse used to give soccer players in her home country. And if you really have the whole day ahead of you, you can languish in the resting room before heading out to restore yourself with a light snack on the first floor.

BARBIER DU RITZ / *Straight razor shave*
15, place Vendôme, 1st arr., M° Opéra, Concorde, Tuileries
Tel.: 01.43.16.30.40

Gentlemen, if you're nostalgic for an open razor and hot towels, or even just curious about getting a simple shave in grand style, then this is the place for you. Joseph, the Ritz barber, has officiated here for ages and has real respect for the old-school way of doing things. You'll emerge clean-shaven and relaxed from this trip into the past. About 150 francs (22,87 €).

BY TERRY / *Personalized cosmetics*
21, galerie Véro-Dodat, 1st arr., M° Palais-Royal
Tel.: 01.44.76.00.76

After her early days at Carita, Terry de Gunzburg joined Saint Laurent where she is now director of makeup production. Her boutique in the galerie Véro-Dodat is her own separate adventure. With a black and deep purple interior, this luxurious headquarters shimmers gently from the sparkle of all the small spherical mercury cases emblematic of the By Terry brand: there are two cosmetic lines, one "made-to-order," the other a "ready-to-wear" version. On the second floor, this sexy forty-year-old has set up her laboratory, a cross between a "color bazaar and a jewelry shop" where hundreds of tints are archived in the rolling panels of an incredible "color library." This is where Terry develops her rare products—the ones the makeup industry often has to abandon due to high costs—without cutting any corners. 2500 francs (381,12 €) and several "fittings" later, you'll leave with an annual supply of base customized to your exact skin type—a caprice to which numerous people, including businessmen regularly covered by the media, have succumbed. Terry's entire science is essentially the art of invisible cosmetics—she is a master of the art of softening features and adding sparkle. Her pale pink sparkle tint *(Éclat de teint rose pale),* an indiscernible device, will guarantee a rested, healthy look for even the most exhausted urbanites.

CHRISTINE SERRES PODOLOGUE / *Pedicure*
26, place du Marché-Saint-Honoré, 1st arr., M° Tuileries
Tel. : 01.42.61.60.00

On the first floor of this pedestrian square, Christine Serres receives her clients in a provincial-looking living room; at the back of her office, an esthetician runs the adjacent beauty institute. Three or four clients chat away while a fourth soaks her feet in a tub of warm water before giving herself over for treatment. Be it calluses or simple beauty care, Christine attacks the problem infinitely gently—cutting, filing, sanding—and finishes up with a creamy massage. You'll emerge with a smooth heel and winged feet. 210 francs (32 €).

COLORÉ PAR RODOLPHE / *Colorist*
26-28, rue Danielle-Casanova, 2nd arr., M° Opéra, Tuileries, Concorde
Tel. : 01.42.61.46.59

Formerly Charlie's right hand man at Alexandre (the legendary Parisian hairdresser)—where he was the special envoy of the king of Morocco's court for ten years—Rodolphe has set up his own business and now all of Paris crowds into his intimate, precious, and magnificent apartment salon. Although the calendar is saturated with appointments, Rodolphe exercises his coloring genius in calm and fine spirits. Articulate and precise, he evaluates with one good look the tints in your hair and your general style, and decides, depending on what kind of woman you are, what change to effect on your tresses, whether it's sweeping brown sculpting coppery henna or simple highlights. You will not leave transformed, but certainly embellished. Don't expect a spectacular metamorphosis: the luxury of this "made-to-measure" color is a subtle question of nuance. Between 650 and 1200 francs (99,10–182,94 €).

ESPACE COMME DES GARÇONS /
Experimental fragrances
23, place du Marché-Saint-Honoré, 1st arr., M° Tuileries

The antithesis of Salons du Palais-Royal Shiseido (see p.105): behind a curtain in blends of pink, all stark white and enameled curves, the office of the Comme des Garçons perfume line is as un-Baroque as possible. In this futurist boudoir, designed by Rei Kawakubo, those adept with experimental fragrances will discover the five new scents of a first series entitled Leaves, as well as different types of aromatherapy candles. A few steps from Colette, this will be a hip spot come Spring.

Chapter 8

LE HAMMAM DE LA MOSQUÉE / *Women's steam bath*
2, place du Puits-de-l'Ermite, 5th arr., M° Censier-Daubenton
Tel.: 01.43.31.18.14

The *hammam* of this Paris mosque is a must—for its exoticism and other-worldly atmosphere of a women's lair. From the vast dimensions and high, decorated ceiling of the resting room (where you can sip mint tea) to the beauty of the authentic Moorish architecture, everything contributes to the sense of disorientation. The only weak point is the lack of an appointment system, so that you are forced to wait and defend your place in line for an exfoliation. The lavish, sweet almond oil massages are given by vigorous and sturdy Moroccan women and will leave you with a sense of total well-being. You'll emerge from here walking on clouds. Around 80 francs (12,20 €).

INSTITUT MARC DELACRE / *For men*
17, avenue George-V, 8th arr., M° George-V
Tel.: 01.40.70.99.70

A real cruise ship luxury, this institute for men cultivates a very male club spirit. The esthetic treatments are approached pragmatically in a four-star clinical atmosphere—all in chrome, leather, glass, sycamore wood, and veined marble. Hair styling, exfoliation, micro-peeling, massage: from the roots of your hair to the bottoms of your feet, including your abs, it's the temple of getting back in shape for stressed-out urbanites worried about finding a new image in a virile environment. An important detail: valet parking at the entrance, shoe shine at the exit.

KEIKO YAMAMOTO / *Vigorous*
8, boulevard de la Madeleine, 8th arr., M° Madeleine
Tel.: 01.47.42.11.96, 06.80.68.08.89

Keiko Yamamoto arrives at your house, sometimes decked out as a geisha, other times looking like a housekeeper returning from the market. It's difficult to fathom the uncommon vigor that has made a legend of this petite Japanese woman. All of Paris gets their treatments from her—master of tea ceremonies, of *ikebana* (flower arranging), of *koto* (Japanese harp), and of *shiatsu* massage. The powerful massage that she administers, finishing with a tiptoe across your back, leaves you in a state of beatitude and overcome with gratitude. Better than an energizing cocktail.

MASSATO / *Masterful hairdresser*
21, rue de Tournon, 6th arr., M° Saint-Germain-des-Prés
Tel.: 01.56.24.03.03

You'll hand yourself over to this highly publicized Japanese hairdresser in a superb, half-Baroque, half-Asian, two-story salon. The appointment won't have been easy to get (you have to slip yourself in between two stars), but here you are: saffron-colored armchairs, red velvet curtains, marble…and you'll await the verdict of the master with impatience and apprehension. With brisk, precise snips, Massato does things his own way. And after one look in the mirror, you'll see that yes, it's still you, but a more modern and indeed more becoming version. This transforming cut will have cost you 1400 francs (213,43 €). Take note of the garden outside, where you can apparently get a manicure while sipping coffee at suitable moments.

M. HO, CHEZ SAINT LAURENT / *Pedicure for stars*
32, rue du Faubourg-Saint-Honoré, 8th arr., M° Concorde
Tel.: 01.49.24.99.66

Expect a two month wait for an appointment with this unusual pedicurist to whom Catherine Deneuve and Jeanne Moreau entrust their feet. Monsieur Ho is of Chinese origin, but practices a Western pedicure method. He works "dry," without a preliminary soaking of feet, and kneads each square inch with impressive dexterity. Believe it or not, you will be so proud of your tootsies when you leave that you'll want to exhibit them at the first possible opportunity. Around 420 francs (64 €).

M.Y.X.T. / *Cosmetics studio*
11, rue de la Jussienne, 2nd arr., M° Les Halles
Tel.: 01.42.21.39.80

With its cement flagstones, brick walls, and aluminum mail-sorting furniture, this makeup studio clearly distinguishes itself from the powder-puff atmospheres typical of beauty salons. Damien Dufresnes, studio and fashion-show makeup artist, wanted to make a bold statement that he is different with the rough, concrete decor at this location set back from the street. Iridescent pigments; speckled, fluorescent, super-coverage bases or natural ones; pencils; brushes; powder puffs; eyelash curlers; and more….You'll find a selection of the best professional brands (Il Makyage, Ben Nye, Tryolan) at unbeatable prices (blush is around 80 francs or 12,20 €, lip pencils around 40 francs or 6,10 €). For 350 francs (53,36 €), you can get yourself made up like a star; or with a simple appointment, benefit from a free, thorough consultation with Christophe or Laurent and learn how to obtain that porcelain tint or fiery look you've always dreamed of. It's also one of the few places (along with Colette) where you can get a supply of Carmex lip balm.

SALONS DU PALAIS-ROYAL SHISEIDO/*Perfume palace*
142, galerie de Valois, Jardins du Palais-Royal, 1st arr., M° Palais-Royal
Tel.: 01.49.27.09.09

The Japanese cosmetics company Shiseido gave *carte blanche* to passionate designer and perfumer Serge Lutens when creating their unique boutique, a window of eponymous perfumes, in the sumptuous setting of the Palais-Royal. Between the pagan sanctuary dedicated to the stars and the iris-colored dressing room, this is one of wildest and most precious places in Paris in its esthetic research. The wealth of materials (marble, rosewood, inlaid mosaics), the virtuosity of the architecture (the central staircase unrolls in a curl of bronze and copper), the delicacy of the orchids in their slim vases…weave together with the bewitching fragrances: *Bois de Violette* (violet wood), *Lys* (Lily), *Santal de Mysore* (Mysore sandalwood), *Encens* (incense), *Lavande* (lavender), and *Tuberose criminelle* (Criminal tuberose).

SAMUEL LUGASSY / *Anti-stress*
4, boulevard de Strasbourg, 10th arr., M° Strasbourg-Saint-Denis
Tel.: 01.42.41.21.77

Samuel Lugassy studied in California, returning with a conception of medicine less "academic" than "health business." A dynamic, informal figure, he attacks all your cervical problems, joint pains, and other knots of stress that can cause a stiff neck. A few questions will allow this extremely lucid man to draw up a map of your office and suggest that you change the placement of your phone in order to help you sleep better at night. After a quick checkup, the session proceeds to progressive "adjustments" through super-quick manipulations of your vertebrae, wrists, and knees. Just the thing after several hours in a plane, especially since this chiropractor is mobile and will happily go to your hotel for an appointment.

SHU UEMURA / *Buffet of colors*
176, boulevard Saint-Germain, 6th arr., M° Saint-Germain-des-Prés
Tel.: 01.45.48.02.55

The opening of this cosmetics shop in 1986 with its pared-down design was a historic moment in the history of beauty. This open, luminous space welcomes you to try all the blushes (480 types in all) the way you would sample dishes at a buffet. The minimalist design of the packaging—simple translucent plastic cases—highlights the incredible palette of nuances that you can combine as you wish in customized preparations. Besides the broad selection of textures—creams, powders, liquids—this vast center of cosmetics offers a wide range of indispensable accessories; natural or synthetic-bristle brushes; sponges, powder puffs; and other facial, hand, and body applicators.

SPA TRIANON-PALACE / *Voluptuous self-indulgence*
1, boulevard de la Reine, 78000 Versailles
Tel.: 01.30.84.38.50

A few yards from the enclave where Marie-Antoinette kept her sheep, it's hard to find anything more stylish that the Trianon-Palace hotel spa, situated at the edge of the park of Versailles. Immense bay windows and white marble colonnades confer a soothing clarity upon these luxurious thermal baths that reinforces the feeling of escape. Set up under a skylight, the big swimming pool allows you several laps after a day in the superb Moroccan-inspired tile *hammam*. A mere fifteen minutes from Paris, it's a key destination for a weekend of both getting back in shape and gastronomic delights: after their "Venus" and "Neptune" programs, the most perverse make dinner reservations at Trois Marches, the hotel's three-star restaurant. Between 295 and 625 francs (44,97–95,28 €).

VILLA THALGO / *Ocean breezes and aqua-gym*
218-222, rue du Faubourg-Saint Honoré, 8th arr., M° Ternes
Tel.: 01.45.62.00.20

The risk has paid off for this center that allows you to taste the pleasures of *thalasso* (water) therapy right in the heart of the city. Elya Boutin, in charge of the Villa, is truly passionate about massage techniques—and her enthusiasm accounts for a great deal of the place's success. She personally selected the center's fifteen estheticians for their "fluid" and she regularly records her latest treatment ideas in a newsletter addressed to her clients. Although situated in the basement, the center is surprisingly luminous: a skylight, that opens up in the summer, actually diffuses natural light over the pool bordered in teak where water aerobic classes are held. On the program of the twenty individual booths are water therapy, algae wraps, Jacuzzi baths, and more. For an experience approaching levitation, try the *reiki* massage, a sort of Japanese-style imposition of the hands that will completely relax you.

FOODS, ETC.

Foods, etc.]

A highly-valued little game at dinners throughout the city consists of exchanging the name of your gourmet grocer for those of the baker, florist, or butcher of the hostess. In order not to miss your turn at this "Trivial Pursuit" of Parisian society—and to give yourself a happy excuse to do some shopping—here are the finest spots for bread, wine, coffee, fruit, and other gourmet goods. Aside from the intrinsic high quality of the products, you'll be able to savor the absolute passion of those who make and sell them—often highly colorful characters who contribute greatly to the charm of the city.

MARCHÉ ALIGRE / *A cook's paradise*
12th arr., M° Ledru-Rollin

This modest-sized covered market resembles a country market with its exposed-beam frame. Around the central fountain, in the smoke of the rotisseries where the pigs are roasted, excellent poultry, butcher, and fish shops all face each other as though on a village square. The products are tremendously fresh, and the regulars greet one another like neighbors.

ATELIER VERTUMNE / *Scented bouquets*
12, rue de la Sourdière, 1st arr., M° Tuileries
Tel.: 01.42.86.06.76

This floral studio works largely by special order for individuals and the big fashion houses (Louis Vuitton is a regular customer and Colette often gets supplies here). Its creation: the confection of fragrant bouquets. According to the season, aromatics and herbs (honeysuckle, lavender, rosemary, thyme, and mint) form the scented basis for these brilliant and pure creations in which narcissus, hyacinth, tulips, and tuberoses add delicate touches of color.

BARTHÉLÉMY / *Exceptional cheeses*
51, rue de Grenelle, 7th arr., M° Sèvres-Babylone
Tel.: 01.42.22.82.24

With its veined marble counter and painted tile floor, you would swear this was a bakery. But the characteristic odor is a sign that that you'll find an altogether different kind of treat here: *Monts d'or, vacherins, langres,* rounds of gorgonzola, *saint-marcellins* with *marc de raisins* (an *eau-de-vie* distilled from pressed grape skins)—runny, creamy, blue…. Lovers of cheese swoon in front of Barthélémy's window.

MAISON BENISTI / *North African deli*
108, boulevard de Belleville, 20th arr., M° Belleville

It was love at first sight when we discovered this North African deli one ravenous night. Despite the neon lighting, plastic chairs, and linoleum, this grocery radiates a true Mediterranean warmth. We like the old-fashioned cash register where the owner sits, the chatter of the salespeople, and most of all, the thick and dense *makrouds* (semolina cakes with dates, cinnamon, and grated orange peel) that melt on the tongue and settle their entire sugary weight in your stomach.

BRÛLERIE DAVAL / *Affordable tea and coffee*
12, rue Daval, passage Damoya, 11th arr., M° Bastille
Tel.: 01.48.05.29.46

The entire passage Damoya recently underwent a vast restoration. At number 12, the odor of paint on the walls still struggles against the aromas of teas and coffees. In this specialist shop, the picturesque owner's golden rule is to offer the lowest prices in the city for her selections. Since all the teas behind her counter are 19 francs per 100 grams (2,90 €), her clients can create their favorite blends without an ounce of concern.

COESNON / *The art of cured meats*
30, rue Dauphine, 6th arr., M° Châtelet, Odéon
Tel.: 01.43.54.35.80

For its mythical sauerkraut sold with the gelatin on the side. For its tasty sausages—not the least bit greasy. For its terrines, its blood sausages, its foie gras…. In this place, one recognizes a professionalism and a love of good things that is wonderfully comforting to witness.

DEHILLERIN / *Kitchen warehouse*
18, rue Coquillière, 1st arr., M° Les Halles
Tel.: 01.42.36.53.13

Last vestige of Les Halles from its market days of splendor, Dehillerin is like a museum entirely devoted to the cult of gluttony. In the basement is the copper cookware (ragout bowls, basins, and a battery of saucepans); upstairs is cutlery, cake molds, and so much more. The place is about as cozy as a garage, but wild in the diversity and precision of its equipment. A necessary stop for anyone who loved *Babette's Feast*.

FINKELSZTAJN / *Eastern Europe*
19 and 27, rue des Rosiers, 4th arr., M° Saint-Paul
Tel.: 01.44.61.00.20 / 01.42.72.78.91

Sweets like Viennese strudels, fig and prune squares, Polish *babkas*, hazelnut crisps, and date rolls. Savory finds such as breads flavored with cumin, poppy seeds, or fried onions, tarama with dill, chopped liver or herring, goulash, *klops*, gherkins in barrels. The two Finkelsztajn shops, both bakery and deli, encourage all kinds of excess. With the first decorated in blue ceramic and the second painted bright yellow, it's a visual feast as well—so overwhelming is the profusion of dishes and colors. If you're feeling blue, these central European delicacies, consumed in moderation, are exquisitely comforting at the onset of winter.

GRANDE ÉPICERIE / *World tour of flavors*
38, rue de Sèvres, 6th arr., M° Sèvres-Babylone
Tel. : 01.44.38.81.01

Where can you find Bricourt preserves, Nunez de Prada olive oil, all the varieties of Illy coffee, Turkish delight, de Cecco and Arrigo Cipriani pasta, the owner of Harry's Bar, and much, much more? At the vast gourmet grocery store of the Bon Marché department store with the most cosmopolitan address on the Left Bank, whose wine cellar, amidst several hundred recommended vintages and regional wines, devotes a large space to wines from around the world. You will also find rare champagnes, and a world exclusive: Quinta da Heredias, a forty-year-old port.

MARCHÉ HÉDIARD / *Chic and exotic*
Flagship store: 21, place de la Madeleine, 8th arr., M° Madeleine
Tel. : 01.43.12.88.88

In the spirit of a sixteenth-century *souk* (Arab market), this exotic shop founded in the late 1800s has small baskets full of loose fruits and vegetables stacked on crates in the entryway. Hédiard is a refined and upgraded version of the corner market—a small grocery for a very select clientele. You're sure to find a selection of fresh produce year-round, including garden greens, hand-picked mushrooms, and exotic fruit—red *pitayas* from Columbia, Victoria pineapples from Réunion Island, pink bananas from Martinique, kumquats, and various papayas. The candied fruits are out of this world.

HERBORISTERIE DU PALAIS-ROYAL /
Healing herbs
11, rue des Petits-Champs, 1st arr., M° Palais-Royal
Tel. : 01.42.97.54.68

There are only a few herbalists left in France, for the simple reason that the degree in this ancestor to aromatherapy hasn't been recognized by the legislature since 1941. They don't sell miracles, but simply the healing effects of certain plants in the form of leaves, capsules, and essences for infusions and other concoctions.

IZRAËL / *Vanilla and spice*
30, rue François-Miron, 4th arr., M° Saint-Paul
Tel. : 01.42.72.66.23

Owner Françoise has an uncanny sense of smell. From a whiff of the bottom of a bowl of Raz El Ranout, she is able to recreate an identical mix of spices that is utterly indistinguishable by mere mortals. In her fabulous shop, you will find an incredible selection of spices, peppercorns, oils, and mustards, as well as succulent Corsican and Asian dried meats. And if she's really smitten by you, Françoise might suddenly remember the arrival of a rare kind of vanilla hidden under the counter.

JEAN-PAUL HEVIN / *Chocolate expert*
231, rue Saint-Honoré, 1st arr., M° Tuileries
Tel.: 01.55.35.35.96

This shop front evokes such a luxurious and refined aura that you could almost confuse it with a perfume shop. And in fact, "perfect delicacies," as Jean-Paul Hevin describes them, are made and sold here like precious jewels. Truffles, candies, bars, mixes of dried fruit and nuts, macaroons, *ganaches* (a blend of chocolate, cream, and butter), cakes, tarts, sorbets—you will find cocoa in all its forms here, and in all its states. Gourmets will want to savor the addictive chocolate *millefeuille* pastries, and those who cannot wait for dessert to indulge their vice will perhaps be tempted by the owner's latest creative folly: chocolate-flavored cheese (goat, roquefort, livarot), to be savored as an hors d'oeuvre.

KAYSER / *The next Poilâne?*
14, rue Monge, 5th arr., M° Maubert-Mutualité
Tel.: 01.44.07.17.81

A baker's reputation is often measured by the length of the line in front of his shop. And if that is to be believed, then judging by the Sunday line that stretches out onto the sidewalk on the rue Monge, Kayser's is excellent. All the neighborhood locals swear by his short Monge baguette with its lightly sweetened center, for which we'd gladly cross the entire city. We also like the melting mini-*financiers*, the *madeleines*—and at tea time, the lemon or orange cake.

LEGRAND / *Straight from the vine*
1, rue de la Banque, 2nd arr., M° Bourse
Tel.: 01.42.60.07.12

The Legrand sons and daughters have owned this unusual wine cellar for four generations in what was a neighborhood grocery store before passing into their hands. Since then, the Legrands have cultivated their specialty: they return from their frequent trips with a selection of vintage wines that they follow closely from year to year, always with the same great attention to quality, in the same way they select whiskies. Dried meats, country preserves, and olive oils, as well as candy, ginger bread *(pain d'épice)* from Dijon, and chocolate are also available to tempt hungry stomachs and to add to the decor. And on the subject of decor, you will notice the cork mosaic on the ceiling: it's Lucien Legrand, the third by that name, who glued his wine corks up there one by one during the scorching summer of 1976 when clients were few. They've been there ever since.

MARIAGE FRÈRES / *Teahouse*
30, rue du Bourg-Tibourg, 4th arr., M° Saint-Paul
Tel. : 01.42.72.28.11

In 1854, the tea trade route passed through Shanghai, Amoy, Hong Kong, Canton, and Macao with a destination of Le Havre. That year, Henri and Edward Mariage, inheritors of a family tradition dating back to Louis XIV, founded a teahouse in the heart of the Marais. Today, the main shop is virtually a historic monument. The salesmen in their white linen jackets are formal and the place resembles the set of a Colonial-era operetta. Antique tea chests from China, scales, sifters, the woodwork of the cashier's nook—everything has remained intact. The selection of crops from Asia, Asia Minor, Latin America, Africa, and the South Sea Islands is simply mind-boggling. The museum on the second floor, furnished with armoires and Chinese consoles, abounds in rare and precious objects; lacquer, rosewood, and Indonesian chests; silver, porcelain, pottery, and cast-iron boxes. It will make you want to go off on a voyage of your own. The most elegant brunch in Paris is to be found on the first floor under a skylight, with deep cane armchairs, exotic plants, and Venetian-style paintings.

MASSIS BLEUE / *Dried fruits and feta cheese*
27, rue Bleue, 9th arr., M° Cadet
Tel. : 01.48.24.93.86

The entire Greek and Armenian community knows this gourmet grocery store for its abundant selection of dried fruits (from dates to pears), different kinds of feta, and honey-flavored Asian pastries served in generous portions. The products are of excellent quality, the salespeople charming, and the alcohol considerably less expensive than elsewhere.

À LA MÈRE DE FAMILLE / *Sweets from long ago*
35, rue du Faubourg-Montmartre, 9th arr., M° Grands-Boulevards
Tel. : 01.47.70.83.69

At À La Mère de Famille, they used to give away a miracle lotion for the eyes free of charge, a recipe handed down by a nun who came to hide in this grocery store from the hordes of the French revolution. Dating back to 1761, this shop's interior has remained unchanged since 1900. A century later, you'll find homemade chocolates, *ganaches*, pralines, and orange-flavored truffles (a specialty)—all made that day or the day before, since the owner is unwilling to preserve them artificially. You'll salivate at the sight of the regional sweets (*bêtises* from Cambrai; *calissons*—lozenge-shaped candy made of ground almonds—from Aix; bergamots), the hand-made preserves flavored with bananas and pineapple, and various treats that must also have been a source of delight to our grandparents.

MILLE FEUILLES / *Petals and objects*
2, rue Rambuteau, 3rd arr., M° Rambuteau
Tel. : 01.42.78.32.43

Transform a restaurant into a French provincial farmhouse, the Garnier opera house into a rose garden, create a Russian New Year's Eve lit by candle-light: these are the sorts of orders that this florist, well-known in film and fashion circles, regularly receives. The boutique—where sweet peas, ane-mones, arum lilies, poppies, and buttercups mix with homey items such as cherubs, planters, pitchers, and votive candleholders—has the feel of a well-tended and ill-assorted collection of decorating knick-knacks. No exotic flowers, but seasonal flowers with poetic harmony: pale and brilliant pinks, subtle oranges, soft and vivid greens....

MILLE PÂTES / *The best of Tuscany*
5, rue des Petits-Champs, 2nd arr., M° Palais-Royal
Tel. : 01.42.96.03.04

Without a doubt the loveliest Italian delicatessen in Paris, which you'll enter with mouth-watering curiosity and which you'll emerge from wanting to give a large dinner party for friends. You'll come back again and again for the Tuscan meats (truffle salami, boar's meat, and venison), the best panettoni that you've ever tasted, the by-products of fresh white truffles (risotto and cheeses), the exclusive wines from Piedmont, and—for nights when the cupboard is bare at home—the delicious homemade antipasti to go.

LES PAPILLES / *Fine wines and terrines*
30, rue Gay-Lussac, 5th arr., M° Luxembourg
Tel. : 01.43.25.20.79

A cross between a wine cellar and a gourmet grocery store, this place is a few years old and already it's become legendary. The owners, a bit brusque when you first meet them, improvised a culinary business to their liking. It's thanks to customer demand that they decided to open their kitchen on Tuesday and Thursday evenings. It's just that you obviously want to linger in this place with its warm Provençal tones and contemporary spirit, where all the wines (some 250 vintages), alcohol, preserves, duck terrines, half-cooked foie gras, olive oils, and other regional products have been scrupulously selected and tasted. Lovers of great wines will be in familiar territory here and neophytes in search of an enlightened selection can easily avoid errors of taste. If you choose not to eat on the spot, it's just the place to gather the ingredients for a sumptuous picnic.

POISSONNERIE DU BAC / Paris's best fish shop
69, rue du Bac, 7th arr., M° Rue-du-Bac
Tel.: 01.45.48.06.64

You'll notice this little fish shop for its navy blue storefront with blue and green scales, and for the crowd pushing its way in on weekends. It's known throughout Paris for its top quality bass, scallops, and *saint-pierre* (John Dory)—essentially, the best the sea has to offer.

POUJAURAN / Divine croissants
20, rue Jean-Nicot, 7th arr., M° Latour-Maubourg
Tel.: 01.47.05.80.88

Poujauran bought this beautiful nineteenth-century bakery in the mid-seventies. Marjolaine, the son of a baker from Landes in southwestern France, wanted to open a "clean bakery" during the first movements toward organic food, which he did—with long hair and some fifty regular clients. Twenty years and several food scandals later, Pourjauran is still loyal to his commitments to public health and sells over a thousand country loaves (*pains de campagne*) daily, as well as *fantaisies*, shortbread cookies, cinnamon cookies, and a variety of crisp and golden pastries that overflow from little wicker baskets. His blends of millstone-ground flour, the pure filtered water used for his dough, and the perfect rise of his bread make him the favorite baker of Catherine Deneuve and Philippe Noiret. And it is said that his succulent *galettes des rois* were shipped once for the Paris-Dakar automobile rally.

À LA POULARDE SAINT-HONORÉ / Return from the hunt
9, rue du Marché-Saint-Honoré, 1st arr., M° Tuileries
Tel.: 01.42.61.00.30

The old, painted facade still displays the phone number "Opéra 10-92," and announces that you'll find first-rate poultry here ("*Volailles de premier choix*"). The front resembles a hunting-scene still life: pheasants, hares, and wild rabbits all hang from hooks on the wall. The time to frequent this unique butcher shop is obviously at the height of game season, when it is assiduously visited by Parisian restaurateurs.

Chapter 9

STÉPHANE SECCO / *Perfect desserts*
112, rue de Belleville, 20th arr., M° Jourdain
Tel. : 01.47.97.18.75

This former collaborator of Christian Constant and part-time associate of the Costes brothers decided to start his own business a year ago. To lure customers, he staked his success on simple pastries such as *chiboustes* (layered dough, soft meringue, and apples flavored with calvados, seasonal fruit charlottes and marvelously bittersweet chocolate tarts that give new meaning to the concept of indulgence. His individual *bûches de Noël* (traditional Christmas cakes shaped like logs) are a hit, and his name never fails to come up at Parisian dinner parties when dessert is served, a fine thing for a baker from Belleville who shouldn't waste any time before setting up shop in other parts of town, especially close to the well-to-do avenue des Ternes.

CAVES TAILLEVENT / *High-tech wine cellar*
199, rue du Faubourg-Saint-Honoré, 8th arr., M° Ternes
Tel. : 01.45.61.14.09

Some stylish women wear cheap baubles and leave their precious jewels in the safe. In the same spirit, you'll find only dummy bottles on the first floor of the famous Taillevent cellars—the some forty thousand real bottles, from the rarest to the most well-known, being kept in storage in the basement under ideal conditions for temperature and hygrometry. On the first floor, a specially arranged cellar offers some thirty vintages at under 40 francs (6,10 €) that one can try every Saturday during a very chic tasting session.

TAVOLA / *Timeless dishware*
19, rue du Pont-Louis-Philippe, 4th arr., M° Hôtel-de-Ville
Tel. : 01.42.74.20.24

Your head will spin when you learn that all the plates, soup bowls, tea sets, and coffee services found here could have belonged to your grandmother, or even great-grandmother. The two antique dealers who opened this store put all their talents into unearthing dishware from the eras of Napoléon III, Old Paris, and the thirties—specifically tracking down pieces that have maintained their fresh look over time and that stand out for their modern workmanship. The Saint-Louis colored crystal stem glasses don't look a bit dated, and you would swear that the eighteenth-century opaline plates are the latest creation of a contemporary designer. As for the prices, they don't hold any awful surprises.

VELAN / *Curry and incense*
83-87, passage Brady, 10th arr., M° Château-d'Eau
Tel. : 01.42.46.06.06

You'll be swallowed up into the passage Brady and will feel you've been transported to a market street in Bombay by the simple evocative power of its smells. In the midst of an increasing number of Indian restaurants, the Velan grocery store remains a one-of-a-kind spice counter. Curry, mace, nutmeg, cumin, curcuma, powdered or stick cinnamon, and chutney— imported from Rajasthan, Goa, and Madras and packaged in little plastic bags—in all, some fifty spices are sold here at unbeatable prices. We also like the Nag Champam incense, sweet as cotton candy, and the orange-blossom-flavored water.

VERLET / *Subtle aromas*
256, rue Saint-Honoré, 1st arr., M° Pyramides
Tel. : 01.42.60.67.39

This minuscule tearoom and roastery is a welcome refuge at the end of a frivolous morning of shopping. Served in fine porcelain, with an assortment of candied fruits and orange sticks, you'll savor the coffee here with your eyes shut to better take in its rich aroma. Flavors from Guatemala, Ethiopia, Columbia, and Mexico.... The menu is dreamy, and the setting, all old wood-work, is both serene and warm.

Walks]

Even if you walk around Paris looking up at the sky to avoid missing any of the architectural details, we too often forget that the city is not made exclusively of cut stone, slate, and concrete—but also water and greenery as well. Real oases in this urban landscape, parks, gardens, and other green surfaces offer smells, light, emotions, and sensations that will help you to better understand the city and to escape it for a while so that you can dive back in refreshed.

MUSÉE ALBERT-KAHN / *The world in a garden*
14, rue du Port, 92100 Boulogne, M° Boulogne-Pont-de-Saint-Cloud, bus 52, 72, 126
Tel. : 01.46.04.52.80 ▪ Open from 11 A.M. to 6 P.M.; closed Mondays ▪

More than one taxi driver will prove his ignorance if you ask him to take you to the Musée Albert-Kahn, but you can also reach this peripheral address by bus; upon arrival, you'll be astonished that this marvel is so little known. There is of course the incredible collection of films shot all across the world at the request of this enlightened banker, including trembling images of Tokyo and Bénarès in the twenties that you'll view on small individual screens. But your enthusiasm will peak when you discover the genius landscaping of the park. On four hectares conforming to Albert Kahn's will, you'll find Japanese, English, and French gardens; a blue forest and a Vosges forest; a marsh; and a fruit orchard come rose garden. At the end of this cultural and multi-sensual voyage (the aromas of each vegetable type are most distinctive in early fall) on the terrace of the retro palm-tree greenhouse, you can sip hot or iced tea, depending on the season, always served with tasty little snacks (coconut cookies or house-made tuile cookies). A real pleasure.

PARC ANDRÉ-CITROËN / *Magical park*
15th arr., M° Balard
Access via the André-Citroën quai or rues Leblanc and Saint-Charles
▪ Open from 8 A.M. to 6:30 P.M. ▪

Designed by trendy landscaper Gilles Clément on the former site of an automobile factory, this is one of the last—and most intelligent—major parks of Paris. Depending on your mood, you can choose to isolate yourself in one of the six thematic gardens (gold, silver, red, orange, green, or blue), lovely little aromatic botanical inlets built on the slopes. Or you may feel like going for a stroll along the rivers vibrant with minerals, sinking yourself into the fallow "scrub" to end up in the middle of the southern zone sheltered by one of the high teakwood greenhouses. Or you can simply lie down in the immense rectangular lawn at the center and stare up at the sky, distracted from your daydreams only by the cries of children playing with the hundred sprinklers that spray intermittently from the square like a pod of whales. A magical spot.

Chapter 10

PARC DE BAGATELLE, BOIS DE BOULOGNE /
Roses and peacock feathers
16th arr., M° Pont-de-Neuilly, bus 43, Porte-Maillot
Access via the allée de Longchamp

Millions of roses—full, delicate, and noble—and more than a thousand varieties line the grounds of this park like a debutante ball. Come spring, the flowerbeds are simply ravishing. And if rose season is over, you can obviously think of Ronsard ("And she lived as long as roses do, the space of a morning...") and cross the vast lawn to venture into the undergrowth, a pretty stroll punctuated by ponds, bridges, panoramic vistas, and artificial waterfalls—where red fish and peacock feathers complete the ideal natural decor imitating art—and at the far end of the park, a lovely pond called the Water Lilies. In May, the iris garden is a magnificent blanket of blues and mauves.

PARC DE BERCY AND MÉTÉOR MÉTRO /
The Seine from above
12th arr., M° Cour-Saint-Émilion
Access via the rue de l'Ambroisie, rue François-Truffaut
▪ **Open from 8 A.M. to 5 P.M.** ▪

Established in 1994 on the site of some abandoned warehouses used once-upon-a-time for wine storage, this wide park is appealing for its simplicity. It is a pleasure to stroll under the plane trees with no other goal than to be in a natural environment, watch the Seine from the height of the terrace, and be taken by the hand over the crosswalk to reach the "romantic garden" articulated around a canal and small ponds. If the walk makes you thirsty, you can finish it off by going as far as the lovely terrace of the Vinea Café, completely isolated at the far end of the cour Saint-Emilion. Don't miss taking the metro to leave the area, as the excellent #14 line is a fun ride. It's imperative that you get into the front of the train, which is glass-fronted with no driver; you'll imagine you've climbed aboard a ghost train, forging ahead at top speed through the subterranean tunnels.
Vinea Café, 26, cour Saint-Émilion; tel: 01-44-74-09-09. About 250 francs (38,11 €).

BOIS DE BOULOGNE / *A turn about the lake*
16th arr., M° Porte-Maillot, Porte-d'Auteuil, Porte-Dauphine

The inevitable meeting place for Sunday joggers, the lake of the Bois de Boulogne can also be appreciated by the idle—who can languidly settle in an old-fashioned wooden rowboat rented for the occasion. Certainly a delight for tourists, but one that Parisians of all ages tired of the city enjoy just as much when they cast off. If your turns about the lake keep you until evening, you'll witness the lighting of the Chinese lanterns at the Chalet des îles, the only restaurant situated on the island and smack in the center of the lake. You can get there by ferry, taking yourself for a Fitzgerald character joining a party from another era as you cross. On this minuscule bit of land where rabbits frolic, the terrace of the restaurant is divinely relaxing in the summer months under a starry sky, in this serene and lovely setting. The obvious romantic quality of the place makes it especially propitious for lovers' dinners far from the hum of the city.

Dinner at the Chalet des îles, on the lake; tel: 01-42-88-04-69. About 300 francs (45,73 €).

PARC DES BUTTES-CHAUMONT / *Lawns for lounging*
19th arr., M° Buttes-Chaumont, Botzaris
Access via the rue Manin, rue Botzaris
- **Open from 8 A.M. to 6:30 P.M.** -

Typically Haussmann in style, this is one of the loveliest parks in Paris. We like it above all for its lawns open to the public (quite the exception in Paris) and so steep that you scale its sides as though off for a picnic in the Alps. Ideal for lazy afternoons (you can settle yourself down here for the entire day, fortified by a snack and a good book), it's also fun with its grotto hung with fake stalactites and its walkway suspended over the lake. Come evening, when the park's gates are closed, the doors of the Pavillon Puebla remain open for a very romantic dinner in the midst of the greenery.

Pavillon Puebla, entrance at the corner of rue Botzaris and avenue Simon-Bolivar; tel: 01-42-08-92-62. About 300 francs (45,73 €).

CANAL DE L'OURCQ – MK2 QUAI DE SEINE /
Peaceful strolls
Canal de l'Ourcq promenade up to the park of La Villette
MK2 movie theater, 14, quai de la Seine, 19th arr.; M° Stalingrad, Jaurès

Following along the Canal de l'Ourcq, you can reach the park of La Villette, one of the only parks in Paris open twenty-four hours a day. In nice weather, have breakfast on the lovely terrace—not to crowded early in the day—of the MK2 movie theater, and follow the thread of water as far as the gallery de l'Ourcq in the heart of the park. This stroll can also be done at sunset, ending at the Prairie du Triangle, where the open-air film festival is held during the summer months. In front of the inflating screen, the rented lawn chairs are spread across the grass for a giant picnic under the stars. One of the busiest and most festive nocturnal meeting places in July and August.

COULÉE VERTE / *A perfect escape*
M° Bastille, Gare-de-Lyon, Ledru-Rollin, Daumesnil
Start at the corner of the avenue Daumesnil and Ledru-Rollin; several entrances

A railroad transformed into a green hillside...the idea is actually quite poetic. Trenches and overpasses covering over two and a half miles travel the length of the 12th arrondissement. Level with the Viaduc des Arts on the avenue Daumesnil, the walk feels like a garden suspended between buildings, at times overhanging the greenery east of the city. The more athletic can pursue this adventure as far as Paris's ring road, where an underground passage gives you direct access to the Bois de Vincennes.

JARDIN DU LUXEMBOURG / *A must*
6th arr., M° Luxembourg
- **Open from 8:15 A.M. to 5 P.M. in winter;
7:30 A.M. to 9:50 P.M. in summer** •

It's impossible to come to Paris without indulging in a walk through the Luxembourg gardens. Poignantly melancholic in the fall when the chestnut trees are turning, almost exotic from May to October when the date palms, pomegranate trees, and bay trees come into full bloom, as joyous as Vivaldi's spring, the "Luco" is the most sentimental of Parisian gardens. The disorder of the chairs, lushness of the flowered grounds, sails of children's little boats coasting along in the pool, lovers facing one another: the princely splendor of it mingles with the comfortable and casual charm of this perpetually animated garden. Don't forget to stop by the monumental Médicis fountain, set a bit apart between the boulevard Saint-Michel and the rue de Médicis, shaded and curiously unknown by lots of Parisians—it's magnificent.

CHAPELLE NOTRE-DAME-DE-LA-MÉDAILLE MIRACULEUSE / *For contemplation*
140, rue du Bac, 7th arr., M° Sèvres-Babylone

A real pilgrimage, this chapel hidden at the end of an alley off the very chic rue du Bac is one of the most cosmopolitan sites in the city. Italians, West Indians, Africans, Poles, old ladies of the 7th arrondissement, jokers of the world come here every day to receive communion from the cult of the Virgin, culminating on August 15th with some twenty thousand faithful spilling out onto the street. Largely represented on the colored tiles of the sanctuary, it is said that Mary appeared before sister Catherine Labouré in 1870 and gave her the task of having a medal made in her effigy. You can still acquire this precious amulet endowed with miraculous powers and, even if an apparition fails to appear, enjoy the extraordinarily fervent climate here.

MUSÉE RODIN AND ITS GARDEN / *Open-air statuary*
77, rue de Varenne, 7th arr., M° Varenne
**Tel.: 01.44.18.61.10 ▪ Open from 10 A.M. to 5:45 P.M.;
closed Tuesdays ▪**

Do you get claustrophobic at the thought of going inside a museum? If so, the garden of the Rodin museum was designed with you in mind. Between the pool and the foliage, you will be able to admire *Les Bourgeois de Calais* and *La Muse Whistler* while contemplating the facade of the magnificent eighteenth-century hotel where you might just as easily not set foot, preferring to bask on a bench in the shade of the garden.

JARDINS SAINT-VINCENT / *Pocket-sized garden*
18th arr., M° Lamarck-Caulaincourt
Access via the rue Saint-Vincent
▪ Open from 8 A.M. to 5 P.M. ▪

An ecological garden before its time, this little patch of green doesn't obey any landscaping plan: it was the pure result of nature in action on an abandoned field before being adopted by the inhabitants of the neighborhood and maintained by the City of Paris. The result: a vegetal tangle as much fun as playing hooky from school—and as wild as a tropical jungle. Kids reign here in this unconventional playground, and you can certainly astonish them by pointing out the inhabitants of the forest: an amphibious webbed triton spends his happy days here and makes for a very presentable version of the Loch Ness monster.

Working out]

If there's a city that makes little room for the body, it's Paris. However, from the solitary jogger to organized roller blading outings, the urban athlete no longer has to wait for the weekend or a vacation to enjoy a bit of exercise. Whether it's an environmentally friendly way to get around or an antidote to stress, working out in all its many forms is gaining ground. In winter, from 6 A.M. on, the silhouettes of runners pierce the fog on the banks of the Seine, and each evening, Parisians go off to learn salsa or the basics of relaxation therapy. Here are the places you can go to move, pump iron, or—more prosaically—purge yourself of toxins after a late night out.

BASE NAUTIQUE DE LA VILLETTE / *Oxford style*
15, quai de la Loire, 20th arr., M° Jaurès, Stalingrad
Tel.: 01.42.40.29.90

To taste the joys of synchronization in the open air, give yourself swimmer's shoulders and the thighs of a cyclist all while remaining seated in the base of a row boat. Saturday mornings, the river banks are still deserted and the small portion of the Seine on the Canal de l'Ourcq is all yours. All you need to do is sign up a week ahead of time—spots are rare—to benefit from a free boat and try (alone, in a pair, or as a foursome) the joys of rowing. From the banks it looks infantile, but the subtleties of holding the oar in real Oxford style require some training. Once acquired, you will glide along swiftly; you can even improvise races on the water. Aches and good spirits guaranteed.

BLANCA LI / *High-tech tango*
7, rue des Petites-Écuries, 10th arr., M° Château-d'Eau
Tel.: 01.53.34.04.05

Known for her bold choreography—in *Macadam-Macadam* she directed bikers, hip-hop dancers, and skaters—this pretty, pale Andalusian has finally created the center of her dreams. It was quite a performance, since the "floating" floor equipped with an Air Floor system like those of the American Ballet in New York and the Royal Ballet in London, had to be shipped over by boat from Texas. Just above New Morning, the two vast, clean, blue studios—made even more vast by the addition of mirrors to the high ceilings—welcome amateurs and professionals for flamenco classes. If you lack a Latin soul, try Rachel Boismene's bar and stretching class—it's very gentle. Around 80 francs (12,20 €) per class.

BOWLING DE L'AVENUE FOCH / *For a stylish strike...*
2, avenue Foch, 16th arr., M° Charles-de-Gaulle-Étoile
Tel.: 01.45.00.00.13

It's all disco balls and music club atmosphere starting at 11 P.M. in this stylish little bowling alley, meeting place of expat New Yorkers. From the shoe rentals to the fifteen practice lanes everything is perfectly maintained, a welcome change from the grimy atmosphere of most establishments of this type. 25 francs (3,81 €) a game during the week; 32 francs (4,88 €) on weekends.

BOWLING DE BOULOGNE / *...and a family-style one*
Jardin d'Acclimatation, route du Mahatma-Gandhi, 16th arr., M° Sablons
Tel.: 01.53.64.93.00

This alternative to the underground bowling alley at the avenue Foch gets its charm from the very pretty terrace on the edge of the Jardin d'Acclimatation. Come summer, the prospect of a drink outside in the sunshine before heading back in to improve your score compensates for the lack of animation in the twenty-four neon-lit lanes. 36 francs (5,49 €) per game.

CENTRE DE DANSE DU MARAIS / *Dance à la carte*
41, rue du Temple, 3rd arr., M° Hôtel-de-Ville
Tel.: 01.42.72.15.42

An incredible atmosphere reigns here in the evenings, when the silhouettes of the dancers look like Chinese shadows in the lit windows and the music and sounds of tapping echo in the cobbled courtyard. Far from the typical ascetic gyms, this magnificent private mansion offers, in the heart of the Marais, a joyfully disorienting experience after a day at the office. Amid the dozens of classes offered—classic, jazz, modern, tango, rock, Oriental dance, Baroque—we opted for Eneida Castro's class. With her short hair with blond highlights, this energetic Brazilian leads her pupils with the discipline of a ballet master rarely found in amateur classes. Over the course of an hour and a half—half bar, half choreography—she works all your muscles with exercises set to the rhythm of her husband's percussions. With a few classes under your belt, the sways and lifts will no longer hold any secrets, and you'll be ready for Carnival in Rio. Around 90 francs (13,72 €).

COMPAGNIE BLEUE / *Out-of-this-world gym*
100, rue du Cherche-Midi, 6th arr., M° Saint-Placide
Tel.: 01.45.44.47.48

Of course we're not going to pretend that this is an unknown address. As TV icons of the eighties, Véronique and Davine built this fitness center on their notoriety. The fact remains that the place, decorated by designer Kristian Gavoille, is absolutely superb. The vast entrance, resembling the lobby of a major hotel, leads directly into the main room, slightly lowered and incredibly spacious. A raised gallery bordered by a guardrail holds the relaxation room (a small amphitheater with red velvet curtains and blue-tinted lighting), the body building room, and the fabulous green-tiled changing rooms. The place smells of incense, essential oils, and a certain kind of luxury. The show biz crowd mixes with the real world—Véronique's bar class boasts more or less regular visits by ballet star Patrick Dupont.

PARIS À ROLLERS / *Group skate*
Gathers every Friday night at 10 P.M., place d'Italie, 13th arr., M° Place-d'Italie

Paris is quite proud of this event: every Friday evening, more than twenty thousand skating fans leave from the place d'Italie, forming a dense and fluid human ribbon that threads its way through the city streets at great speed. The immense popularity of this group skate means that it is now accompanied by squads of police officers—some of them wearing skates themselves—who ensure safety by blocking traffic at each intersection. International in scope (people come from California to participate), this "city-skate," whose route changes every week, is in theory open to amateurs. In reality, the exhilarating experience of this nocturnal trip across Paris is best attempted as a group so that you can hold each other's elbows—and hands occasionally—especially on the descents. Called "a societal phenomenon" in urban legend, this gathering has even piqued the interest of sociologists.

PARIS À VÉLO C'EST SYMPA / *Bike tours and rentals*
37, boulevard Bourdon, 4th arr., M° Bastille
Tel.: 01.48.87.60.01

Michel Noë, a Belgian who arrived in Paris in the early nineties, started looking for work—on his bike. It required a fair amount of imagination and nerve to transform this circumstance into a business. But when he launched his first city-wide bike excursions in 1993, he was instantly successful. A few miles of bicycle-friendly routes later, the idea grew in scope. Michel Noë has a spacious location and is now accompanied by a riding guide on all his outings. "Heart of Paris," "Strange Paris," "Markets of Paris," "Literary Paris": with gradual inclines and real slopes, each itinerary has its own monuments, atmosphere, smells, anecdotes, and breaks. For those who are not fans of group outings, the idea can be adapted to the individual. It will cost you 80 francs (12,20 €) for the rental of a sturdy bicycle for the day without the official commentary; 170 francs (25,92 €) for the guided tour.

PISCINE DE PONTOISE / *Evening swims*
19, rue de Pontoise, 5th arr., M° Maubert-Mutualité
Tel.: 01.55.42.77.88 ▪ Hours vary depending on the day ▪

In the heart of the Latin Quarter, this 1930's swimming pool retains the spirit of a private club despite the fact that it's open to the public. With its tiled walls, changing rooms with individual cubicles overhanging the pool, and natural light filtering through the skylight, it's one of the last pools with charm in Paris. We particularly appreciate its evening hours—Monday through Friday from 9 P.M. to midnight. About 25 francs (3,81 €) for the entrance fee.

ROLLERS ET COQUILLAGES – NOMADES STORE / *Roller blade rentals and lessons*
39, boulevard Bourdon, 4th arr., M° Bastille
Tel. : 01.42.72.08.08

Two steps from the Bastille, this is one of the biggest French stores specializing in roller blades, with some 130 types ranging from 500 to 4000 francs (76,22–609,80 €) and close to 200 pairs available for rent. Ideal for a three-step initiation: first, take two or three hours of lessons with a certified teacher to master a basic practice course followed by some outdoor training; second, rent a pair of skates (which you can change as often as you want during the rental period); third, meet up every Sunday morning at 11 A.M. for the Rollers et Coquillage outing leaving from the store—easier than the one organized on Friday nights by Paris à Rollers (see p. 132).

ROLLER SPIRIT / *Roller dancing*
4, rue Étienne-Marcel, 2nd arr., M° Étienne-Marcel
Tel. : 01.42.21.91.98

All white and blue, with armchairs draped in black and small low tables, this roller blade shop (open until 9 P.M., Sundays included) does not cultivate the pinball-machine esthetic so often adopted by its colleagues. With Jamiroquai playing in the background and high gym-style mirrors, this shop—that both sells and rents—hopes to appeal to on-line dancers. Covered with three layers of asphalt plus two of shiny polish, the floor "grabs well," so as to allow amateurs to play at Holiday on Ice. Originally from the nightclub world, the owner—with his ponytail and big smile—hopes to gather people here who just want to have a good time; he has all sorts of top-secret festive events up his sleeve. Rentals: 60 francs (9,15 €) during the week; 70 francs (10,67 €) on weekends.

TAI CHI-CHUAN, JARDIN DU LUXEMBOURG / *Breathe in...breathe out...*
6th arr., M° Luxembourg
Tel. : 01.49.83.71.27 (martial arts headquarters)

Sunday mornings, the Luxembourg garden fills up with strange figures with flexed legs, tense with attention. Antoine Ly, master of kung fu, teaches his art to citizens in search of balance in the midst of the trees and Sunday joggers. Flexibility, self-control, strategy: tai chi requires less physical strength—the principle consists of using that of your adversary—than concentration. Very educational, master Ly uses the language of images, happily employing metaphors to pass on a bit of the Eastern spirituality of his art. Early mornings in the Luxembourg Gardens are chilly in spring, but "without the cold of winter, there would not be the smell of Japanese cherry blossoms." An entire philosophy, to be followed by an old Bruce Lee movie....

KIDS

Kids]

You've got it all organized: museums, shopping, eating out. You won't even have time to satisfy all your desires. But one little thing slipped your mind when you made these plans: the wishes of your little tots don't exactly coincide with yours. To overcome boredom and bad moods here are some ideas, including excursions for the whole family and kids-only activities. So you'll never again be able to say that Paris isn't a city for kids….

BEAUBOURG ATELIERS D'ENFANTS / *Art for kids*
Rue Rambuteau, 4th arr., M° Rambuteau, Hôtel-de-Ville, Les Halles
**Tel. : 01.44.78.12.33 ▪ Open from 11 A.M. to 9 P.M.;
closed Tuesdays ▪**

Your little genius may just be the next Picasso. Kids can express their artistic talents in the children's activity studios at Beaubourg. Educational and inventive, the activities here may help spark their talents. You won't find any major works of art on the program, but rather drawings, cutouts, and collages designed to hold the interest of kids between the ages of five and ten. When it's time to go, the kids compare their work to that of an exhibited artist—for example, their collage of circles to a canvas by Delaunay—and will be on familiar terms with the mysteries of creation in all its simplicity. It also gives you time on your own to peruse two levels exhibiting a century of modern and contemporary art. 20 francs (3,05 €).

SUNDAY BRUNCH AT DÉTOUR / *Recess in the basement*
5, rue Elvézir, 3th arr., M° Saint-Paul
Tel. : 01.40.29.44.04

It's Sunday, and you'd gladly go have a leisurely brunch somewhere, but what to do with your little tykes? Just bring them along—since the Détour transforms its club space into a child-care center that day (proof that night owl parents have aged a bit!). In this basement playground, kids can leaf through books of cartoons, play with the counselors, make new friends, and watch magic shows. It will cost you 100 francs (15,24 €) for brunch, plus a supplement per child. It's best to phone ahead to confirm, since this formula is appealing but still in its infancy.

CAP VERNET / *Gastronomic initiation*
82, avenue Marceau, 8th arr., M° Alma-Marceau, Charles-de-Gaulle-Étoile
Tel. : 01.47.20.20.40

Kids have terrible taste: they love awful toys, disgusting candy, and they consider a hamburger to be the height of culinary refinement. This time, you've decided to awaken their senses to more sophisticated and mature pleasures by bringing them to a "real" restaurant. They are already making faces, but the dear little ones don't know about this godsend: for 75 francs (11,43 €), they will consume the same menu as you (who will pay about 200 francs or 30,50 €) and have the right to play at the table. Every Saturday and Sunday at lunchtime, in addition to a lighter bill and meal, the under-twelves get to sniff at little bottles—pineapple, leather, toast—from a box of scents made available to them.

Chapter 12

LE DIVAN DU MONDE / *Children's theater*
75, rue des Martyrs, 18th arr., M° Pigalle
Tel.: 01.45.43.29.67

One Sunday each month, the kids go swing at the Divan du Monde, with or without Mom and Dad. On the program: snacks, grenadine, and fruit juice, and a performance led by Imbert and Moreau—a couple of pros in children's theater. The words are kind (but not sickly sweet), and the melodies pass from rock 'n' roll to twist, from French Cancan to the Charleston and the Polka. The kids let themselves go, dancing and laughing, and generally leave carried away by this special party designed especially for them. Take note: it's jam-packed on Halloween. 60 francs to enter (9,15 €).

LES ÉTOILES DU REX : LE GRAND REX /
Movie studio tour
1, boulevard Poissonnière, 2nd arr., M° Bonne-Nouvelle
Tel.: 08.36.68.05.96 ▪ Open from 10 A.M. to 7 P.M. Wednesday through Sunday; departures every five minutes ▪

This Alice in Wonderland tour of the film industry begins by taking you behind the scenes and ends on the screen. Setting off in a big glass elevator, the public crosses the room and starts its tour behind the scenes with a visit to the producer's office. Along the way, you learn a few things about sound effects (the echo of a wooden box for the steps of King Kong, the vibrations of sheet of metal to imitate thunder), almost get pecked by an oversized hen—and all this time, you are being filmed without even knowing it! It all ends with a showing where you can dream that you're a star between two cuts of cult films. "Very good," according to Zöe, aged ten. 45 francs (6,86 €); for kids under twelve, 40 francs (6,10 €).

JARDIN D'ACCLIMATATION / *Nature and culture*
Bois de Boulogne, 16th arr., M° Sablons
Tel.: 01.40.67.90.82

A real amusement park that can be enjoyed as a family, on the back of a pony, or on a boat ride along the artificial river. Dozens of athletic activities (car races and mountain bikes) and cultural ones (culinary and chemical labs for experiments) are on offer. We have a weakness for the fun mirrors and the big canvas trampolines—it's simple, free, and always entertaining. Don't hesitate to take your kids through the Musée en Herbe, a playful and intelligent activity museum whose exhibits introduce the littlest ones to painting—from prehistoric to Picasso. During the summer, the recently renovated wooden terrace next to the Pavillon des Oiseaux (the vast aviary) offers an appealing setting for a drink and a snack. Park entrance fee: 13 francs (2 €).

JARDIN DES PLANTES ET GRANDE GALERIE DE L'ÉVOLUTION / *Natural history museum*
36, rue Geoffroy-Saint-Hilaire, 5th arr., M° Censier-Daubenton, Jussieu
Tel.: 01.40.79.30.00 ▪ Open from 10 A.M. to 6 P.M.; closed Tuesdays ▪

As sensitive souls, we'd rather open the cages of the zoo of the Jardin des Plantes than gaily throw peanuts to their hosts. However, after a tour of the gardens and their two greenhouses, we didn't miss the spectacular set of the Grande Galerie de l'Evolution in the Museum d'Histoire Naturelle, Paris's natural history museum. Featuring a whale skeleton, stuffed wild cats, parades of animals worthy of *Fantasia,* monkeys hanging in full swing, myriad insects pinned like precious jewels, and more, these animals seem to be more full of life than the ones in the zoo! An absolute must, no matter how old you are. Entrance fee: 40 francs (6,10 €).

JARDIN DES TUILERIES / *A well-filled day*
Rue de Rivoli, 1st arr., M° Concorde, Tuileries

A must for tiny tots: pony rides around the Jardin des Tuileries. Between the Louvre and Concorde, trotting around statues by Rodin, Carpeaux, and Giacometti, this fairy-tale tour enchants children. To be followed by a turn on the merry-go-round, and pushing sail boats on the pond (they can be hired on the spot). The afternoon flies by until teatime, with fruit juice on the terrace of the Café Véry or hot chocolate at Angelina's on the other side of the rue de Rivoli.

PARC DE LA VILLETTE / *Recreation center*
26, avenue Corentin-Cariou, 19th arr., M° Porte-de-la-Villette, Corentin-Cariou
Cinaxe, tel.: 01.42.09.86.04 – Géode, tel.: 01.40.05.12.12

Undoubtedly one of the most exciting recreational centers in Paris. An immense park dotted with theme gardens and the red follies of Bernard Tschumi, this is a real land of adventure and discovery—and an assured success as far as the kids are concerned after a showing at the Géode or the Cinaxe. In the huge polished steel ball with reflecting geometric patterns, a gigantic hemispheric screen envelops the audience—who are lightly inclined in their seats—giving the impression of being "inside" the film. You'll leave feeling a bit dizzy, and with your head spinning with images. Inspired by technical advances in aviation, the Cinaxe hall simulates the movements of the action and pins the audience, seatbelts fastened, to their seats. Kids love it. Given the crowds on weekends, you will have to wait a bit between buying your ticket and the showing, often booked up in advance. To kill some time, head over to the Dragon—an immense slide set up in the park—or the windmills with pedals in the Garden of Dunes (open-air activities that are much more fun than those offered by the Cité des Sciences, which are a bit outdated). Adults: 57 francs (8,70 €); children: 44 francs (6,71 €).

Services]

Problems with hems, zippers, visas, latent colds, or other untimely nuisances? We've anticipated these little worries and chosen a few addresses designed to take care of these and other inconveniences rapidly and efficiently. To this list of indispensable services, we've added a few frivolous ones, so that you will be perfectly comfortable when it's time to book seats at the opera, order a taxi for the next day at dawn, or buy flowers for a lovely stranger.

ALLO MAMAN POULE / *Babysitting*
7, villa Murat, 16th arr., M° Porte-de-Saint-Cloud
**Tel. : 01.45.20.96.96 ▪ Open Monday to Friday from 9 A.M. to
7 P.M.; Saturdays 10 A.M. to 7 P.M ▪**

This babysitting agency is the salvation of parents who like to go out
without fretting. The young women who are sent to you are subjected to
an extremely rigorous selection process. Rates for a minimum of three
hours: 36 francs per hour (5,49 €) for the babysitter, 60 francs for the agency
(9,15 €). Subscriptions possible upon request.

ALOC / *Computers*
141, boulevard du Montparnasse, 6th arr., M° Vavin
Tel. : 01.55.42.90.34

An indispensable service in this day and age for you and your colleagues. In
case of breakdown (or theft), Aloc offers PCs and Macs for a minimum of
forty-eight hours at a rate of 500 francs, tax included (76,22 €).

CORDONNERIE VANNEAU / *Shoeshines*
45, rue Vivienne, 2nd arr., M° Grands-Boulevards
Tel. : 01.45.08.17.98

More unusual than street shoeshiners, and more comfortable. Regally set-
tled into magnificent raised armchairs, you can scan the newspaper and sip
coffee while the shine is restored to your shoes. If you're pressed for time,
you can leave your shoes and pick them up later.

COOKING CLASSES BY FRANÇOISE MEUNIER /
Get to your ovens
7, rue Paul-Lelong, 2nd arr., M° Bourse, Sentier, Les Halles
Tel. : 01.40.26.14.00 – fax : 01.40.26.14.08
fmeunier@easynet.fr – http://www.lntweb.com/fmeunier

In small groups, learn to create an appetizer, main course and dessert
(French cuisine) under the kind supervision of Françoise Meunier. At the
end of class, you get to feast on the meal you've prepared. Table arts and
wine accompaniment round out the three hours spent in the company of
this culinary expert. A guided visit through the old halls of the Montorgueil
market is available on request. 500 francs per class (76,22 €); five classes:
2000 francs (304,90 €); ten classes: 3800 francs (579,30 €).

Chapter 13

DREAM TEAM / *Theater seats*
Tel.: 01.53.98.97.53 – fax: 01.53.98.97.52

Whether it's for Don Giovanni at the Garnier Opera house or Notre-Dame-de-Paris at the Palais des Congrès, Dream Team is the specialist in last-minute theater tickets. Prices upon request.

FNAC / *Books and CDs*
74, avenue des Champs-Élysées, 8th arr., M° Franklin-Roosevelt
Tel.: 01.53.53.64.64

A sudden craving for music after dark, the latest bestseller, or the newly restored version of *The Umbrellas of Cherbourg* video? Go straight to the FNAC on the Champs-Élysées—it's open until midnight.

GENTLEMEN PILOTS / *Escort service*
10, place Vendôme, 1st arr., M° Tuileries
Tel.: 01.53.45.54.40 – fax: 01.53.45.54.55

For when you don't want to go out alone in the evening. A male escort that you select via catalog will hold doors open for you and keep up conversation for an evening at the opera, a wedding, or even a shopping trip.

MALLES BERTAUX / *Luggage repairs*
135, rue d'Aboukir, 2nd arr., M° Sentier
Tel.: 01.42.33.03.80

This Parisian institution specializes in luggage repair, whether you need to have a zipper replaced or your old Vuitton trunks buffed and shined. If it's urgent, the personnel really does its best to accommodate you.

MARIVAUX / *Theater seats*
7, rue de Marivaux, 2nd arr., M° Richelieu-Drouot
Tel.: 01.42.97.46.70 • Open from 11:30 A.M. to 7:30 P.M •

The Marivaux agency has been a point of reference for lovers of opera and theater since 1932. The charming Claudia always has very good seats available for her clients, and sometimes manages miracles....

MICHEL CORNUBET / *Chauffeurs*
22, rue de Courcelles, 8th arr.
Tel.: 06.09.16.59.31 / 01.43.59.14.34

You may not be able to afford a full day's services of this chauffeur of billionaires, who's always up to date on the best addresses for antiques and contemporary art. Don't be piqued. Cindy Crawford herself was told "no" one morning when she called—too late—to reserve. Perhaps you could indulge in the luxury of these limousines for a simple transfer between the airport and your hotel. From 650 francs (99,09 €).

NESTOR SERVICES / *Tailoring, dry cleaning*
Tel. : 0801.630.600

No more clean shirts, or the hook in a pair of slacks needs to be sewn up right away? Nestor Services offers a pick-up and delivery service for all your sewing and laundry needs. Express dry cleaning (24 hours) and touch ups (48 hours); shirt: about 22 francs (3,35 €); pants hook: 40 francs (6,10 €).

OFR SYSTÈME / *Magazine stand*
30, rue Beaurepaire, 10th arr., M° Republique
Tel. : 01.42.45.72.88

Photography, design, graphic design, fashion: absolutely all the most specialized international magazines can be found here—*Intramuros, ID, Dutch, Wallpaper, Purple,* etc.

PHARMACIE LES CHAMPS / *24-hour pharmacy*
84, avenue des Champs-Élysées, 8th arr., M° Franklin-Roosevelt
Tel. : 01.45.62.02.41

At the far end of the gallery, a pharmacy that's open 24 hours a day, seven days a week.

PHARMA PRESTO / *24-hour pharmacy*
Tel. : 01.42.42.42.50

An indispensable service when you're stuck in bed with the flu and your best friend is off strolling on a beach in the Seychelles. Pharma Presto will bring you your prescription within the hour with a simple phone call, 24 hours a day, 365 days a year, for an average of 250 francs (38,11 €).

POUYANNE TRADITION / *Dry cleaning*
28, avenue Franklin-Roosevelt, 8th arr., M° Franklin-Roosevelt
Tel. : 01.43.59.03.47

Pouyanne is one of the last traditional dry cleaners in Paris. Specializing in the most delicate fabrics, this place will take care of all the work you need done based on an estimate. Don't hesitate to leave your favorite Hermès scarf or your latest pleated pants from Issey Miyake in the hands of these craftsmen.

Chapter 13

PRESSE 24 H / 24 / *24-hour newsstand*
33, avenue des Champs-Élysées, 8th arr., M° Champs-Élysées-Clemenceau
Tel. : 01.40.76.03.47

Undoubtedly the best-stocked kiosk in Paris for international newspapers
and magazines; what's more, it's open 24 hours a day.

RENT YOUR PHONE 7 / 7
116 bis, avenue des Champs-Élysées, 8th arr., M° George-V
Tel. : 01.53.93.78.00

Rent Your Phone, open seven days a week, is undoubtedly the agency that
offers the most high-quality options in the jungle of phone services: BI band
phones, delivery, returns.... In addition, the rental is free, and only your calls
will be billed. National: 7,20 francs/minute (1,10 €); international: 14,40
francs/minute (2,20 €).

TAXI FÉLIX / *Reliable*
Tel. : 06.11.27.30.73

While Parisian taxis don't always have the best reputation, this chauffeur
center will surprise you with its rare kindness and professionalism.

VIP VISA EXPRESS / *Administrative services*
Tel. : 01.44.10.72.72

A last minute trip.... Are you facing visa trouble? VVE will take care of everything with a simple phone call. Between 130 and 250 francs for rush
requests (19,82–38,11 €).

VOGEL LAGNEAU / *24-hour florist*
2, rue de Marignan, 8th arr., M° Franklin-Roosevelt
Tel. : 01.47.23.42.67

Where to find red roses for your lady-love at any hour? This little boutique
on the rue Marignan is the flower headquarters for hotel bellboys who've
known about this place for years. We suggest that you always call ahead to
speak to the charming Madame Vogel.

Index
Index by theme

Index
Index by theme

1st arrondissement

Index

Index by neighborhood

Index